MASSIVE ACTION MARKETING:

How To Grow
Your MLM Business Outside
Your Warm Market

Study Guide

by

RANDY GAGE

Published by GR&DI Publications
7501 East Treasure Drive, Lobby Floor
North Bay Village, Florida 33141
(305) 864-6658

Gage, Randy
Massive Action Marketing Study Guide
ISBN 1-884667-11-2

ISBN 1-884667-11-2

Re-orders:
Gage Research & Development Institute, Inc.
1-800-432-4243   (305) 864-6658

Introduction

It's my belief that most people fail in network marketing because they work too hard. This business is not easy. It's not supposed to be. But it is simple. Disarmingly so.

Most people in network marketing are on a treadmill - doin' it, doin' it, doin' it - but never secure enough to stop and ask: "What am I doing and why am I doing it?"

Hopefully, the work I do will change that for you. I've labored the last five years on developing resources to not only get you out of the rat race, but make sure you don't replace it with the network marketing rat race. It is my hope that the resources I've developed (like this Study Guide) will help you stop working in your business long enough to work on your business.

My experience is that we make it too hard. Because the traditional ways of making a living are, for the most part, quite hard - we almost feel guilty if success comes too quickly for us. So we make it hard. Which makes it harder for our people. Yet, if we stood back and analyzed what we do, we'd find that we have unnecessarily complicated a very simple, fun business. If we stay focused on the basics, follow them persistently and keep ourselves duplicatable - success comes quite readily in a two- to four-year time period.

This book is my contribution to that process in you. I want you to build as fast as practically possible - yet, not in a way that prevents your organization from duplicating your success.

Since conducting my three $5,000-a-person-Bootcamp weekends - I've been deluged by requests for an affordable version for the average distributor who's not yet making a large income. I've refused up to this point, because I couldn't come up with a way to keep it duplicatable.

After months of study, application and soul searching (not to mention the valuable input of audiences in Boston, San Francisco, Los Angeles, St. Louis and Chicago), I feel that I can finally do that. This Study Guide and the accompanying album are the result. I believe students of my *How to Earn at Least $100,000 a Year in Network Marketing* series can now use these resources to go to the next level. Where the first series showed you how to construct a complete, duplicatable system - this series will allow you to exponentially expand your market, yet, do it in a way that's congruent with your system.

Network marketing brings to the marketplace products and services that would never make it there by conventional means. Our empowering business structure is rescuing millions from the savage, dog-eat-dog mentality of the corporate world. And our opportunity for true economic independence is freeing people from the bonds of indentured servitude that most jobs have become. We are offering people a chance to truly create their own destiny.

Your job is to spread the light of this amazing and empowering business. My job is to help you do that more effectively. You're the real hero in that process - never lose sight of that. What you do does make a difference.

You are never sponsoring someone into your program, but actually offering them the opportunity to build - and live - the future of their dreams. If anything I teach you helps you to do that more effectively - then we've both done a good day's work. Because the work you do is important. It's important to you; it's important to your loved ones; and yes, it's important to the world. For if you raise the consciousness of one family, you increase the prosperity of the entire community. Let it begin ... with you!

Randy Gage
November 19, 1996
Miami Beach, Florida

What You Need To Know First

We know that the most important question you face is duplicatability. Can the things you do to build fast, be readily duplicated by the people in your group? How can you grow quickly without sacrificing your group's ability to duplicate you? Is there a way to build faster - that empowers them to build faster as well? These are the issues we must look at.

I feel like Dr. Jekyll and Mr. Hyde. On one hand, I'm known as "Mr. System" - the guy who preaches about having a complete, step-by-step duplicatable system that anyone can follow. My *How to Earn at Least $100,000 a Year in Network Marketing* teaches exactly how to do that, and it's become the best-selling album in the entire industry. I've helped companies all over the world set up systems that their distributors can duplicate.

On the other hand, it was John Milton Fogg who dubbed me "the man who put the marketing back in network marketing." As an entrepreneur for a couple of decades - and a continuous self-study program - I've learned a great deal about how to make money with marketing. My copywriting and other skills have been upheld by the court of last resort - the marketplace.

I've built large distributorships and I've helped thousands of others to do the same thing for themselves. I've helped billion dollar companies launch network marketing divisions, and perhaps more rewarding - I've helped start-up companies build the system and create the foundation that is even now taking them to billion dollar status. Along the way, I've come full circle.

I began my career working my warm market of friends, neighbors, relatives and casual acquaintances. Then, I began to explore the avenues of cold market recruiting - building by mail, display ads and classifieds. I saw a tremendous increase in my personal group as I refined these strategies.

It provided a big boost in income as my group volume increased greatly and I was working with a large number of direct lines.

What I discovered was that these increases were not being passed down the group in depth. Quite simply, my people could not write copy, design ads and purchase mailing lists with the effectiveness I could. My top people - working as hard or harder than I was - were not able to earn the money I was making. I saw a dramatic drop-off in width as my organization got beyond the tenth level.

I gradually evolved back to my warm market, but tried to incorporate sound marketing principles which would allow me to build faster. It is this precise balance between growing big - fast, and remaining duplicatable, that we seek here. We don't want you to grow any slower than is possible. Yet, we don't want you to pay the price of stagnant growth on the lower levels by practicing strategies that don't readily duplicate hundreds of levels down.

It is your job in this first segment to decide how far you will venture into the cold market strategies we look at in the later sections.

You will learn how to write copy, select mailing lists, design ads, craft headlines and build by mail. You will discover strategies that will literally let you sponsor dozens of people a month. Yet, I hope you won't use them in this way ...

Instead, it is my hope that you will learn the marketing principles behind these strategies and apply them to building your warm market. Here's what I mean:

Some of the techniques we'll discuss are easy, inexpensive and quite easy to duplicate. Others (like building by mail) are not very duplicatable.

Yet if you can learn the principles behind writing good copy - you will make the best presentations and present the best meetings you've ever given in your life.

If you can craft a good headline - you'll know how to open a presentation. If you learn how to write "bucket brigade" copy - your prospects will eagerly await the next part of your presentation. If you really understand the difference between features and benefits - you'll know how to slice through a prospect's apathy and skepticism so they understand that your information is important to them.

It is your choice. You can use my techniques to look like a hero by building a large personal group fast. Or you can really be a hero by staying duplicatable, building a little slower initially, but ultimately teaching many others how to build a large group.

I'm hoping you'll choose the latter and base all your decisions on the same criteria the Iroquois Indians did. When an Iroquois tribe faced an important choice, the village leaders got together and asked themselves "When we make this decision - how will it affect the seventh generation of children?" And that was the most important consideration.

Not how it affected them, or even their children. But rather, the seventh generation of children.

If you make your choices, not on how they will affect you - but how they'll affect your seventh generation distributors - you are certain to follow a program that many thousands of people can duplicate. And isn't that what we're all about?

_____ training can be deadly.

You need to know <u>what</u> you do and <u>why</u> you do it!

What is your mission? _____

_____

_____

_____

_____

_____

_____

_____

_____

What is your Unique Selling Proposition (USP)?_____

_____

_____

_____

_____

_____

_____

_____

_____

_____

You cannot _____ the market - you must let the market _____ you.

Always look at things from the prospect's point of view - then test.

_____ ads produce a positive result only for the mediums they are run in.

(Put your money into actions and mediums that bring you a return on your investment only. "To keep your name in front of people" is not a valid justification to spend your time, money or resources.)

_____   _____ transcends all.

People will always desire ultimate benefits like security, health, recognition, etc. The definition of these desires will change, but the underlying desire will not.

NOTES

NOTES

NOTES

NOTES

Marketing Mastery Fundamentals

These 11 fundamentals form the underlying basis of all the marketing processes I teach. Most are interrelated. Most of them also apply to building a network marketing organization in a duplicatable way. A few of them don't, but I've included them for the sake of completeness.

Mastering these fundamentals will give you the ability to market any legitimate product or service in any industry. In the companion set of audiotapes, I've attempted to explain the relationship of each fundamental skill to network marketing and where each falls on the scale of duplicatability.

Study these fundamentals well and use them as a checklist to come back to as you plan any marketing ventures.

You're a marketer - not an _____,

_____ or _____.

If I notice how cute or how clever your ad is - I have missed the message.

Tell the whole story - _____ your

prospect.

Give your prospects all the information they need to

make the right buying decision for them. Don't sell;

don't convince; don't close - <u>educate</u>!

Resell and re-establish _____ value.

Actual value is absolutely irrelevant when faced with the prospect's perceived value.

You must lead with the _____ and substantiate with the _____.

If you're talking about you, your company or network marketing - you're talking features. If you're talking about the prospect - it's a benefit. Features are important, but only to establish credibility of the prospect's benefits.

Marketing style and medium must be _____ with your product or service.

The average director line will be worth half a million dollars over the life of your business. When your business makes over $100,000 a year - it will be valued at about a million dollars. Are the marketing materials you use - and the image you project - congruent with a million dollar business?

Evaluate each marketing _____ as you would a distributor.

If you do not measure results - you cannot improve them. When you know what activities don't work - you can drop them. When you find what works well - you can do more of it.

Savvy marketing is based upon offering _____ than your competitors.

Give people a clear, defined and unmistakable reason to do business with you. Once they know it's in their own best interests - you don't have to sell, simply educate.

Make it _____ to do business with you.

If it's risk free to do business with you - or "better-than-risk-free" - why wouldn't people do business with you? Reverse the risk.

Bonuses or incentives are a _____

_____.

Premiums, freemiums and other incentives can be the deciding factor to push your prospect over the top. They can increase both the perceived value of your offer, and the actual benefit the prospect receives.

Never lose an opportunity to _____,
_____ and _____.

Remember when you were a child and you opened your presents on your birthday, Chanukah, Christmas, etc.? Weren't you glad when you discovered that the salesperson had cross-sold some batteries to go along with your new toy? At least 40% of the people provided an additional offer at the time of purchase will usually accept it.

Marginal net worth or lifetime value.

Once you know what it costs you to _____
a customer, and the _____ _____
of that customer - you're indestructible!

Now, do the same calculations for getting a new <u>dis-tributor</u> instead of a customer. Don't be afraid to invest in your business and don't be dissuaded by less-than-perfect early results. Stay in and the long-term benefit to you will be extraordinary.

NOTES

NOTES

NOTES

NOTES

Prospecting For Profit

Many people say, "I like network marketing; I just hate to prospect." That's like saying you like to eat - you just don't like to chew. Prospecting is the lifeblood of your business. Without it, your network would atrophy and die.

So why don't most people like it?

I believe this is because they really don't understand what prospecting really is and inadvertently make it more difficult than it really is.

Most people getting involved with network marketing think they are entering a sales business. This simply isn't true. They are entering a distribution business, one that is creating a complete paradigm shift in the way products and services get to the end consumer.

Now, obviously, marketing is involved, for why are these consumers selecting these particular products? But the reality is that most of what we do in this business is education about our product services, not selling per se.

Think of the products that have gained mass public acceptance through network marketing: pynogenal, enzymes, antioxidants, vitamins, and non-toxic, environmentally-friendly soaps and cleaners. Products like these would not sell initially were they on a shelf at a supermarket or health food store. The interesting thing is that today - such products do sell on a supermarket shelf. But that is only possible due to the educational efforts performed by millions of network marketers over the years.

Even today, network marketing is the home of many other products that need to be conversationally marketed. It's hard to imagine a customer going to a store and selecting Oxyfresh toothpaste, Melaleuca dishsoap or Envion's programmed nutrition meal bars.

They simply wouldn't know the story behind them - and why they are such a good value. Likewise the family financial services from Freenet or the discounted long distance services. We are an industry with some amazing products - products not conducive to "selling" to people - but products which "sell" very well to an educated consumer.

Successfully building a network falls within a similar kind of situation. Very little lasting success is achieved by the people who practice strong sales skills and sell a large number of distributorships. They invariably have big personal groups, yet very few people making money. Usually they have just one other person (if any), approaching a livable income. In addition, they almost never have any real growth in depth, and virtually never have width below the ninth or tenth level.

Conversely, the people with poor sales skills, but proficient in <u>teaching</u> skills do quite well in this business.

Once they learn their company's system, they set out to teach it to the people they sponsor - then teach them how to teach their own people. This process is duplicated down the organizational structure, creating both depth and ever-expanding width.

So in both arenas - distributing the product and building the organization - teaching and training are the most important things. <u>The people who do best in the business are not the super salespeople</u>, but rather, <u>the good teachers</u>.

So how does all this apply to prospecting?

Most people join a program and say, "Who am I going to sell this stuff to?" and, "Who am I going to get to sell this stuff?" Then, mentally, they start discarding dozens of people from their prospect list because they're not sales types.

They shy away from calling people on their "chicken list," fearing (probably rightly so) that those people wouldn't be interested in selling products.

So by failing to realize that this is not a sales business - most distributors never approach the people most likely to be successful in the business. This perceived handicap ("Most people won't want to do this business because it's sales.") becomes an actual one.

This doesn't have to be the case.

Here's what we know. When you approach the business from the teaching standpoint and follow a duplicatable system - virtually anyone with desire can do the business. In fact, you will have more people who need the business than you can actually work with.

This changes the whole equation ...

When you realize that you can only work with two or three people at a time, you approach the entire situation differently. You recognize that many, many people would benefit from your products, and just as many need your business opportunity. In fact, with corporate downsizing, economic factors, and 500,000 jobs a year becoming unnecessary due to technology - the need for our business opportunity increases daily.

Now the questions to ask are, "Who are the two or three people I'd like to help first?" and, "Who would I like to sponsor that I would enjoy teaching and traveling with to the exotic resorts of the world?"

You start to see prospecting as a screening process ...

One in which it appears your prospects need what you have to offer much more than you need them. In actuality, it is a win-win situation for both of you.

The most important part of the equation is not "Who can you get?" but "Are they willing to be helped?"

Here's what I mean:

You will find that prospecting people need not be a challenge. The real challenge is using your time in the most effective manner. It doesn't make sense to try to sell network marketing to someone not at the appropriate consciousness. Many people are not happy - but they are satisfied with the way things are. They may not enjoy their work or their life - but they are not motivated to do something about it. They slog along in their life of quiet desperation, lamenting their fate, yet unwilling to take a stand for themselves.

They once had dreams, but they have buried them far from their conscious mind and everyday thoughts. We can't help these people at this time ... because they don't have a dream. This is where the screening process comes in.

You don't want to be making presentations to people without dreams. Or to people who may have dreams, but have negative pre-conceptions about network marketing and don't want to be confused with the facts. This brings only rejection and negativity - and who needs more of that?

That's where a pre-approach packet comes in.

This is a literature packet designed to give to prospects before they receive a presentation.

The purpose is to decide if they should even get a presentation.

Ideally, the pre-approach packet should open with the benefits of the business (unlimited income potential, tax breaks, being your own boss, empowering others). By the prospect's response to this, we can determine if they have a dream.

The pre-approach packet should also make it clear that the method we're proposing to achieve those dreams is network marketing. So, if the prospect has a closed mind about networking - you can find out about it at this point.

This packet should also be a teaser, meaning <u>it shouldn't make a presentation</u>. Rather, you want it to lead a qualified prospect to a presentation — and lead an unqualified prospect away from a presentation.

In essence, here's what a good pre-approach packet will do:

It should let the prospects know there's a better way to live; it hopefully will interest them in this better way of life; it lets them know they will only get the benefits described from network marketing; and it lets them know that to find out more - they need to make an appointment and sit down with the person who gave them the packet.

If your company has such a pre-approach packet - great. But as a rule, I don't like company materials, but generic ones at this point. Remember, this is pre-approach - which means "before the approach." I like generic materials because there is an implied third party endorsement.

I've created a beautiful generic package called the *Lifestyle Freedom Pack*. It's a combination of my *Escape the Rat Race* audiotape and my Special Report, *Money for Life*, packaged in a "lifestyle" type album. This is being used with great success around the country.

If you're constructing your own packet, here are some materials to consider:

Are You Walking Past Fortune? - a brochure by Tom Schreiter [1]

Money, Money, Money, Money, Money - a booklet by John Milton Fogg

The Greatest Opportunity In the History of the World - a book by John Kalench [2]

Business is Booming - a booklet by Michael S. Clouse [3]

Remember, you don't need to "sell" anyone anything. We like to say, "We're looking for people who are looking." Use a pre-approach packet to sort through the people you talk to. Find the two or three or four out of ten who have a dream and are willing to do something about it. Then, and only then, move those people to the next step of the process - an actual presentation.

Prospecting is not cold calling strangers or trying to set up phony bonding situations with people you meet in the shopping mall. It's just going about your life - living more life - and just being open for people who are looking for more. Don't chase them, don't beg them, and most of all, don't sell them. Expose them to the proper information and let them discover whether the business is right for them.

1. Available from KAAS Publishing: (713) 280-9800
2. Available from Gage Research: 1-800-432-4243 or (305) 864-6658
3. Available from Upline: (804) 979-4427

Qualifying Questions:

"Have you ever thought about opening your own business?"

"Do you ever look at ways to increase your annual income?"

"Have you ever thought about developing a second income stream?"

"Do you know anyone who's looking for more money, more time, or both?"

"Would you be interested in a business that can bring you residual income security?"

"Write Your Personal Commercial"

_____

_____

_____

_____

_____

- I'm in the marketing business.

- I help people develop second incomes.

- I'm in network marketing.

- I help people open their own home-based business.

Lifestyle Business Cards

This is the actual card I used when I was still building a network.

Closed   Open

LIMITLESS LIFESTYLES

RANDY GAGE

• Limitless Income
• Time to enjoy it
• Exciting Travel Opportunities
• Helping others as you help yourself

"Live the Lifestyle of Your Dreams, and help the people you care about do the same."

Suite 53
Miami Beach, Florida 33139

(305) ████████

RANDY GAGE

Lifestyle Business Cards

Here are samples of cards other students of mine have
done:

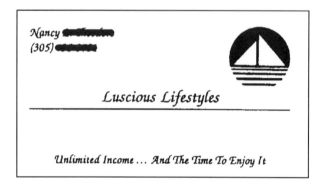

NOTES

NOTES

NOTES

NOTES

NOTES

Creating Compelling Offers

The two things that motivate people are:

The fear of _____.

or

The desire for _____.

Lead with benefits - substantiate with the features.

Target the offer to the _____, not to your interests.

Make sure your offer is a direct pipeline to the desired _____.

Include an incentive for immediate _____.

As you construct an offer, make a list of the benefits the prospect receives from your product or service. Then, make a list of the <u>hidden</u> benefits.

Benefits	Hidden Benefits
_____	_____
_____	_____
_____	_____
_____	_____
_____	_____
_____	_____
_____	_____
_____	_____
_____	_____

Compare the Offers

$49 = Distributor Kit

$49 = Distributor Kit

Forms you need to do the business

Training segments

Product description

Get-started training

Conference calling

Monthly counseling

Open meetings

Company training events

Newsletter

Help with presentations

NOTES

NOTES

NOTES

NOTES

Getting No-Cost / Low-Cost Publicity

The biggest challenge faced by radio and TV talk show producers is:

To find good _____.

They desperately need articulate people who can talk about lively, interesting and controversial topics - like network marketing.

Actual Samples

On the following pages you'll find some actual samples of media coverage-generating tools. First is a sample postcard which we mailed out to program directors nationwide to get radio interviews. A good postcard can generate a number of good appearances.

Next is a sample media release. Notice the key points: Lots of white space at the top, date of release (immediate in this case), and double-spaced type.

Following that is a sample "pitch" letter. This is a letter you send to editors (or producers) of media in which you would like to be interviewed. The key thing you want to do here is show the editor why an article about you would interest their readers.

After that you'll find several copies of actual articles that ran about me. Notice we reprinted them on one page then added our 800 number. We now use these to send to potential clients. These are much more powerful than sending a brochure because of the third party endorsement.

Finally, you will see a copy of a column we syndicate to papers all over the country as a lead-generating strategy for *Entrepreneurs Alliance International.*

GAGE RESEARCH & DEVELOPMENT INSTITUTE, INC.
7501 EAST TREASURE DRIVE
NORTH BAY VILLAGE FL 33141

Your listeners can make money...

(TO FIND OUT HOW, FLIP THIS CARD)

Sample Radio Card (front)

...lots of it
...by using strategies from the right talk show guest!

If your listeners are:

- Interested in making more money
- Small business owners (or would like to be)
- Salespeople
- Looking for a financial change in their life

then book Dale Ledbetter as your next talk show guest.

Dale is more then just an author and professional speaker, he's in the trenches every day, running a multi-Million dollar sales force.

Dale is one of the only people that not only understands how sales works, but can also explain it so that ANYONE can understand. He is a lively guest who knows when to talk, but also when to listen. Dale will provide your listeners with information that can make them more money in their job or their business.

So, what could your listeners expect when you book Dale as your next guest?

They will get lively, innovative information that they can go out and apply immediately, to make more money, no matter what type of business they are in.

Call 800-432-4243 and book Dale Ledbetter today!

When you call to book Dale, be sure to ask for a copy of his new book, The Ultimate Sales Professional.

Sample Radio Card (back)

PRESS RELEASE – PRESS RELEASE - PRESS RELEASE - PRESS RELEASE

For Immediate Release:

Contact: Nancy ~~McDonald (xxx) xxx-xxxx~~

Tampa, FL A revolutionary new concept in network marketing begins this month with the advent of International Self-Esteem (ISE), a Florida based company. ISE is committed to supporting their distributors in the areas of marketing and training with a duplicatable system in place to coincide with their official October launch date. To that end, they've brought on board Network Marketing Guru Randy Gage to set up this structure.

ISE president Nancy McDonald sees this program as a way to rocket her company to a leadership position in the industry. Says McDonald: "If you want the best company, then you need to get the best people. So it just made sense to get North America's #1 Networking Coach on our team. By bringing in Randy, we are showing the same commitment to our distributor network as we put into creating a product that would bring consumers back month after month."

Sample Press Release Format

Gage's role at ISE will be to set up the company training program and developing the audios, videos, brochures and other sponsoring materials to make the distributor's job easier. Other companies that Gage has done programs for include AVON, Sunrider, NRI and Shaklee. Says Gage: "I'm excited to add ISE to our roster of clients. Their strong commitment to their distributors is the stuff MLM success is made of."

ISE is currently in pre-launch operation and recruiting leaders nationwide. The company's mission is to help raise the world's self-esteem - one person at a time. Their flagship product is an "ESTEEM" subscription which includes a beautiful 4 color glossy monthly magazine packed with helpful self-development tips, a 4 tape seminar album and discounts to special live seminars around the country. Besides Gage, some of the other presenters have been Dave Yoho, Louise Hart and Mike Wickett. ISE entrepreneurs earn money from selling subscriptions as well as from an entire personal growth catalog. They can be reached at 1 (███) ███-████.

- 30 -

The Raleigh Group, Ltd.

a visibility marketing company

Mr. Scott DeGarmo, Editor
Success Magazine
239 Park Avenue
New York, New York 10169

September 1, 1995

Dear Mr. DeGarmo:

A company in war-torn Croatia increased their bottom line by half a million dollars last year when Randy Gage custom designed a marketing training program that taught his distributors to reverse the marketing norm and instead **lead with customer benefits and then substantiate it with features.**

A prominent multi-level-marketing magazine increased its bottom line by a half million dollars in only six months when Randy redesigned both his magazine and his direct mail campaign. Using the technique known as *back-ending,* he suggested adding value to the magazine's cache through the creation of meaningful products for the readership, and a resource catalogue that would act as the distribution vehicle. His advice to sell other peoples educational products so he didn't have to spend his own money reinventing the wheel has added handsomely to the mother lode.

A Chiropractic Management company benefited by a quarter of a million dollars in six months when Randy introduced him to the concept of, "What does it cost you to get a new patient in relationship to what that patient is worth to you long term. In other words, knowing what the marginal net worth of a customer is.

One pleased client loves to tell how Randy's coaching has made him an extra 5 million dollars. As Randy put it, "I shared with him a common sense marketing tip garnished with a paradigm shift."

Your audience and their bottom line will benefit from these and many other outrageously profitable strategies when you begin to tap into Randy's wealth of money making case studies.

Who is Randy Gage? He's a business doctor, personal marketing coach, seminar presenter, author and publisher of business books and a catalogue in which to house these valuable tools. And because he shun's the limelight, he's been nicknamed by his clients "the Reclusive Marketing Guru."

At 36 Randy is a living example of just how the American dream

maximize your biz-ability through viz-ability

1223 wilshire blvd., # 502, santa monica   90403   •   voice 310.998.0055 • fax 310.998.0034

Sample pitch letter to generate articles

The Raleigh Group, Ltd.

a visibility marketing company

can come true. A high school drop out, his high six figure consulting fees come from bottom line improvements he designs for both mega companies and individual clients.

As personal coach to thousands, his list of clients and admirers reads like a veritable Who's Who of the appropriate industry.

Four times a year he hosts marketing bootcamps, from the model he instituted as a training program for his own organization, begun just seven years ago.

CEO's take three days out of their busy schedule to attend his $5,000 marketing boot camps so they too can learn how to triple their earning capacity.

What differentiates him from the pack of marketeers is, instead of theory, Randy teaches pragmatic, down-to-earth "how-to's." That's what makes him so sought after. He's on the horizon of high tech, high touch strategies that make him the definitive "how to" expert in the field.

And so you won't forget tomorrow what you learned tonight, there are home study tapes and a catalogue of myriad business books and tapes, including many authored by Randy, offering continuing education tools for, and dedicated to those who understand that improving the mind is a cornerstone to raising income.

You're more than welcome to share the experience by joining us in Hawaii, October 19-22 for a Marketing Bootcamp, a mini entrepreneur seminar in Ft. Lauderdale November 18, or one in Los Angeles December 2.

I look forward to discussing the possibility of an interview with Randy Gage, marketing coach and nice person. I'll call you next week.

Sincerely

Raleigh Pinskey

maximize your biz-ability through viz-ability

1228 wilshire blvd., # 502, santa monica,   0403 • voice 310.998.0055 • fax 310.998.0034

The Network Trainer

$1.00

October/November
1993

The Training Journal for Professional Network Marketers

Spotlight On . . .

A professional problem solver

by Kathie Jackson Anderson

On most mornings, network marketing trainer Randy Gage walks right past his office to grab his bicycle and pedal out into another brilliant Florida morning. With the ocean on his left and the art deco architecture of Miami Beach on his right, 34-year-old Gage knows his lifestyle is a powerful advertisement for the business system he teaches.

Gage lives on a small island between Miami and Miami Beach. His home and his office are in the same building, and while most of us are commuting to work, Gage is bicycling Miami Beach's famous Ocean Drive. Even when he is at work, he is traveling the country teaching the business-building strategies that made him one of the top network marketers in the country.

Gage is at the forefront of those who are bringing 21st century communication systems to networkers.

"Drawing circles in the living room went out with the bee-hive hairdo," he says. "If you want to be competitive in the 1990s, you'll be using technology. Today's top leaders use fax-on-demand, nation-wide conference calls, voice information systems."

Teacher With A Message

Gage's engaging presentations are known nationwide through his seminars and his best-selling audio tape series, *How to Make $100,000 A Year in Network Marketing.*

His warm and inspiring audio tape, *Escape the Rat Race,* is one of the most potent prospecting tools available today.

To all his projects, Gage brings a sly humor and an obvious relish for his work. His message . . . today's leaders are using tomorrow's technology. And you can too.

He is a top example of how network marketing is changing as it emerges into mainstream business circles. Thanks to teachers like Gage, today's networkers are trained, motivated and professional. In their businesses, they're using many of the business-building techniques practiced by any high technology entrepreneur or Fortune 500 company.

They've learned that systems such as voice mail boxes, automated information systems and fax-on-demand services make information — and networkers — available 24-hours a day, seven days a week to prospects without interfering with the lifestyle networkers cherish.

In addition to his seminars, Randy conducts training programs for specific companies such as New Resolution, Shaklee and Forever Living Products, and he specializes

Randy Gage . . . from problem child to problem solver.

in consulting with start-up network marketing companies.

Although he is now living the life networkers strive for, he attained his goals exactly in the way he teaches others to reach theirs . . . he earned them.

"I always say, if I can make it in this business, anyone can," he says, dryly.

Article Reprint

Gage, a Wisconsin native, left home at age 15, a high school dropout. "I was a problem, problem child," he says. "I had a real attitude problem. School, to me, was just the most boring thing."

In his first few years on his own, Gage lied about his age and worked two jobs, both of them for national restaurant chains. "I got excited about the restaurant business," he says. He was made an assistant manager at Howard Johnson's at

"Horrible. I didn't make a dime. I didn't make *any* money for the first five or six years in the business. I tried other companies, and became an MLM junkie. Little by little, I developed my system. I'm not a sales type; I'm a very introverted person. I just kept experimenting and finding what worked. Then I spent another three or four years perfecting the system and another year putting the information together. "I started a supervisor's

Professional Evolution

Gage's work has continued to evolve, moving now into training networkers and networking companies to take advantage of the communication revolution.

"The future will be high-tech," he says. "But it will be high-tech, high-touch. It won't be robots calling up and getting orders. It will be the same person telling his or her story, but to thousands of people by satellite instead of to a few people in one room."

Gage's message to networkers is a familiar one. "Never give up," he says. "People give up in six months if they're not rich. They go back to what they wanted to escape in the first place. What if it took six years like it took me? Who cares? What is six, versus 40 years?"

"There I was, running a $1 million operation at 17."

---

age 16, although the restaurant thought he was older. He made manager one year later. "There I was, running a $1 million operation at 17," he says.

Gage became Howard Johnson's problem-solver. In five years, he moved to 18 cities, taking over problem stores, turning them around, then moving on to the next challenge.

Eventually, he opened his own restaurant and restaurant consulting business. Along the way, a friend introduced him to network marketing. "Man, that was it," he says. "To me, this business was made just for me. I knew it was perfect for me."

And how did the future premier trainer do as a networking beginner?

school for my own group. I scheduled it for the last Saturday of the month. Other groups heard about it and asked to sit in. Then somebody flew in from New York for the training, and that just blew me away. Then someone flew in from California — whoa! — then I got invited to take the seminar to Chicago, and then to New York . . . I never looked back. Teaching has always been my favorite part of the business." Along the way, Gage incorporated personal development techniques into his own life and into his training sessions. "At some point, I began to set aside personal time every day," he says. "When I started doing that, it changed my whole life. I teach in my seminars, that your network can develop only as fast as you do."

Business journalist Kathie Jackson Anderson is co-author of *Future Choice: Why Network Marketing May Be Your Best Career Move*, a groundbreaking new book now reaching fine bookstores nationwide. *Future Choice*, by Anderson and networking success trainer Michael Clouse, is already acclaimed as one of the most powerful recruiting tools in years. For more information contact Candlelight Press, P.O. Box 55455, Seattle, WA 98155, or phone (206) 365-1140.

For more information about Randy Gage's groundbreaking consulting services and seminars, contact, Gage Research at 1-800-432-GAGE.

October/November 1993

Gage Research & Development Institute. Inc. (800) 432-GAGE or (305) 864-6658

The Network Trainer 65

AMERICA'S JOURNAL OF INCOME OPPORTUNITIES

October 1992

"The airlines are bankrupt, the Savings & Loans are in shambles, family businesses are going the way of the dinosaur and the government can't find enough red ink to print the budget. Is there any doubt that the traditional ways of doing business don't work anymore?" So says North America's #1 Networking Coach, Randy Gage.

As network trainers go, Gage is distinctly different. Along the Atlantic Ocean in tropical Miami Beach, he directs the Gage Research & Development Institute. It has consulting, management, training and marketing divisions—all bearing the distinctive Gage brand. Gage has made quite a niche for himself as the trainer's trainer. Yet when FreEnterprise caught up with him, we found a shy guy who often sleeps til mid-day, doesn't own a watch and works in Nike sneakers.

The 33 year old Gage laughs at the irony, but explains it this way. "I've owned many businesses. I've been president of the Chamber of commerce, I've worked for big corporations. I've done the whole "merger mania/ dress for success" scene. I mean, isn't that why we all go into networking to begin with, so we can wear blue jeans and sleep til noon?" And while he may look more like a mystery writer than a MLM guru, looks are deceiving.

What began as a training program for his own organization just 3 years ago has now transformed Gage into a personal coach to thousands. His stable of admirers reads like a veritable Who's Who of the industry.

Shaklee Lifetime Master Coordinators, Bodywise 5 Star Managers, Platinum Executives from Jewel-Way and Executive directors from Sunrider International all look to Gage for the latest innovations on how to build an organization bigger, better and faster. When Avon Products decided to test the MLM concept in the Mid-West, they brought in Gage to make the change from Avon Ladies to networking superstars.

Eager and would-be MLM'ers all over the country line up to take his latest seminar "How to Earn at Least $100,000 a year in Network Marketing." Word of mouth advertising has made it the most popular seminar of its kind. Dean Smith, a lifetime Master Coordinator with Shaklee in the Chicago area explains how

it happened: "When I first heard about Randy's seminar I was quite skeptical because there's been so many training and other things that just didn't pan out. So I went first to check it out for my group. I found it to be the most well organized and presented training I've seen in 20 years in this business." Smith has gone on to bring Gage back for regular Shaklee training programs.

Charles Possick, an industry name for decades sees Randy as the future of networking in the nineties and beyond. Says he: "Randy Gage's tapes and seminars can help anyone become an overnight networking professional. While other trainers teach theory Randy teaches pragmatic, down-to-earth "how-to's" that he learned by building large groups himself. He's on the cutting edge of high tech, high touch networking. While the dinosaurs are still teaching that the only way to build is drawing circles in your own living room— Randy's showing how to use MLM advertising strategies, voicemail training boxes, fax on demand, telephone demand conferencing and training programs that duplicate 50 plus levels deep."

What began as a training program for his own organization just 3 years ago has now transformed Gage into a personal coach to the thousands. His stable of admirers reads like a veritable Who's Who of the industry.

Gage shrugs off the accolades, but it's obvious that he's proud of his reputation as the definitive, "how to" expert in the field. Says he: "We have enough "rah-rah" hype in this industry without me adding to it. I've always believed that if you teach people the specific things they need to know to build a network— they don't need the hype."

He's also quick to point out that anyone can make a 6-figure networking income without special degrees or credentials. Last year he was awarded an Honors Scholarship at the local college. But as often with Gage, looks are de-

ceiving. "Yes I'm proud of that scholarship," he declares, "but I'm even more proud of the fact that I make it in networking as a high school drop-out! It's only because of networking that I could go back, get my GED and go to college. What other career could afford me that time and flexibility?"

While he wears such diversified hats as a consultant to MLM companies, developing success tools, columnist, author and teacher, it's the training role Gage relishes the most. He relates: "Getting across the country and doing my seminar is the most rewarding thing I do. It's where I get to interact one-on-one with the distributors—the real people in the trenches. It's a sad fact, but 95 percent of the people in this industry aren't making any money. Every company has their $100,000 Poster Boys, but for every one of them, there are thousands who aren't making $30. When I can show them that they really can do this—it makes it all worth while."

It was only natural that when FreEnterprise was looking for a training program that they could co-sponsor, they turned to Gage. Publisher Larry Hessick saw the opportunity to broaden the magazine's ever expanding role in educating the industry. Hessick explains the reasoning behind the move: "We've always seen FreEnterprise as a distributor's best friend. Our job is to assist him or her in building their program the fastest, smartest, best way possible. By helping to bring Randy's seminar to the distributors in the field—it gives us a chance to help out own distributor force and "walk our talk" to our many readers."

When Gage isn't teaching people how to build an MLM organization, you'll probably find him riding his bike along Ocean drive or adding to his comic book collection. He describes himself as "happily divorced" and "living the lifestyle of my dreams." The way he sees it: "Everyday I get the chance to help people who are fed up with their careers, dead end jobs or just having a lousy boss. I can empower them and show them a better way. I can give them the one thing they desperately want and really deserve—freedom from the Rat Race. I do what I love and I love what I do. What more can I ask for?"

What more, indeed.

GAGE RESEARCH AND DEVELOPMENT, INC. – 1-800-432-GAGE

Article Reprint

17 Deadly Sins of Marketing

By RANDY GAGE

(MPS) — Asked at Entrepreneurs Alliance International "Empowering Entrepreneurs to Succeed" seminar, this question is so important it could mean the success or failure of your business:

Q. Is it true that all marketing efforts are successful, I just have to do them?

RANDY GAGE

A. No! Here are 17 of the deadliest marketing sins to avoid.

1. Not having a complete understanding of the market. Numbers that will buy? Who needs it? Population locations? Can they pay?

2. You think your prospects are as interested in your product as you are. They're interested only in "What's in it for me?

3. You haven't studied your competition. Know what they're doing, and do it better.

4. Failing to lead with benefits and substantiating with features. Benefits lead with "you get."

5. Not establishing a value. If customers don't know why they have to pay the cost, they won't.

6. Running image ads. They'll deplete your budget and won't bring you responses.

7. Not using headlines. Ads and direct marketing get up to 4,000 times higher response ratios.

8. Not testing and tracking. Why waste money if placements don't draw?

9. Not telling the whole story. Reveal all, and more will respond.

10. Not following up with prospects who don't buy now. If you don't, someone else will sell them the service you could have.

11. Attempting a one-step transaction in a two-step space. "Call for details," rather than packing an ad, gets you qualified prospects to whom you'll give the information that they need for a successful decision.

12. Not telling the prospect what to do. The more you leave to chance, the less people will buy. Have them sign the contract, and give them the stamp.

13. Not using testimonials. Get success stories from those benefiting from your service. Use names a prospect can relate to.

14. Not giving the prospect a reason to act now. If you don't, 80 percent won't. Offer a limited offer.

15. Failing to upsell: Sell product warranties; cross-sell: Sell a workbook to accompany the tapes.

16. Not reversing the risk. Advertise a complete refund,

17. Finding one market method that brings 90 percent of your business and stopping there. Don't rest on your laurels; keep testing marketing strategies.

The next column discusses "How to Increase Your Customers by 20 Percent in One Month." Until the next time, great marketing!

Randy Gage, president, Gage Direct Marketing and Development, is director of Entrepreneurs Alliance International Seminar Division. Join and learn the tools to grow your business and succeed in your marketplace. For membership, benefits and seminars, write EAI, 901 North Point Parkway, Ste. 102, West Palm Beach, FL 33407; 1-407-688-9099. CU964164

NOTES

NOTES

NOTES

Prospecting With Classifieds

Classified Ads:

■ Simple

■ Inexpensive

■ Relatively easy to learn

Not as duplicatable as warm market only - but fairly duplicatable

Classified Tips

- First words in ad are the headline.

- Do headline in bold type.

- Do not run under "Help Wanted" sections.

- Screen calls with an answering machine (respond only to replies with phone numbers).

- Do a basic, but brief presentation on the phone - use this opportunity as a verbal pre-approach step. In other words - use the initial interview to disqualify the non-prospects.

Sample Classifieds

BUSINESS OPPORTUNITY Your own business with unlimited income. Free car, flexible hours. $99, get started now training. Call for details, 000-0000

TEACHING Good teaching skills will earn you unlimited income and the time to enjoy it. Your own business with less than $500 investment. Call 000-0000

FREE CAR, profit-sharing and retirement security in your own business. $200 gets you started now. 000-0000

DOMESTIC ENGINEERS who want to make $$$ in their own PT business. 000-0000

This is an ad inspired by Mark Yarnell of NuSkin in his book, *Power MLM*. I adapted it to meet my particular situation. You can adapt it to your specific circumstances.

Ex: "I think work is for people who don't like to fish..."
" I can ski Mt. Ranier..."

Let Me Describe You:
You have a nice car and a decent place to live.
You're mortgaged to the Max.
You have lots of little plastic cards,
even some gold ones.
You're tired of the traffic on I-95.
You've had no significant vacation
in the last 5 years.
You're winning the Rat Race,
but you feel like a Rat.

Let Me Describe Me:
I have an income in the top 2% of the country.
I spend 2 hours a day in quiet meditation
and self-development.
I can watch the sun rise in Bogota,
and watch it set in Key West.
At 33, I'm semi-retired
helping people like you escape the Rat Race.
For a personal interview:
Randy 000-0000

NOTES

NOTES

NOTES

NOTES

Writing "Killer" Copy

- Take morning self-development time.

- Set goals for the day.

- Take no interruptions.

- Make a list of the benefits.

- Make a list of the hidden benefits.

- Write to one specific person in the target market.

- Never stop when you are in the flow of consciousness.

Must be personal

Create an internal message with bold, italics, headlines, P.S.s and underlining.

Take as long as you need to tell the whole story.

Write in conversational, everyday English at the seventh grade level.

For letters:

- Always use a headline.

- Always use a salutation.

- Always use a signature.

- Always use a postscript.

8 Keys to a "Killer" Letter

1. An envelope that begs to be opened.

2. A headline that commands interest.

3. An opening paragraph that lets the reader know in no uncertain terms that this letter is important to him or her.

4. A "bucket brigade" flow that pulls the reader through the pages.

5. A feeling that the reader is being brought "inside" a place, product, event or cause.

6. An overall feel that this is a letter, not a mass mail piece.

7. A Post Script that intrigues the reader to read or re-read the copy above it.

8. An "internal message" that gives the "Readers' Digest" version of all the above.

Rules for Copywriting

1. Never lie.

2. If you make a claim, prove it.

3. Lead with benefits; substantiate with features.

4. Personalize.

5. Make sure any slang or jargon is familiar to the reader.

6. Reveal a minor flaw.

7. Give copy news value.

8. Write the way real people talk, not English professors.

9. Never talk down to your audience. Look them in the eye, or look up to them.

10. Ask for the order.

11. Make it easy for the prospect to buy.

12. Give an incentive to act Now!

13. Substitute "You" for "I" whenever possible.

TONY CANNESTRO
President
Business Manager

ROBERT C. BELANS
Sec.-Treas.
Business Agent

8350 N. W. SEVENTH AVENUE
MIAMI, FLORIDA 33150
Phone: 691-8440 Area Code (305)
1-(800) 253-3452 Outside Dade County

AFFILIATED WITH INTERNATIONAL BROTHERHOOD OF TEAMSTERS

My back feels better . . .

Dear Local 769 Member:

A short while back, I wrote you encouraging you to see chiropractic physician, Robert Hochstein, if you or a member of your family was in pain.

Little did I know that the person getting help would be me . . .

I've been suffering from headaches, stiff neck and sore shoulder muscles for some time. Also, occasionally, my back would "go out."

Brother Clarence Lark from Local 390 urged me to follow my own advice and see if Dr. Hochstein and Chiropractic care could help me.

The results . . .

Instant relief of my headaches, my neck and shoulder muscles have loosened up, and my back feels better.

And that is why I'm writing you again.

I recommend every person in Local 769 to see Dr. Hochstein. At my request, he has agreed to give a complete consultation and examination free of charge to the Local 769 members and their families. I urge you to take advantage of this free offer.

To schedule your free exam, call (305) 654-9797, and let them know I sent you and tell them you are in Local 769. The Chiropractic Care Center is located at 441 and County Line Road, minutes from anywhere. Please don't put up with symptoms or pain needlessly like I did – go in and get your free examination.

To your good health,

Tony Cannestro, President

P.S.   Dr. Hochstein's office is open Monday through Friday until 7:00 p.m.

BETH ROYALL
National Marketing Director

Ref: The nationwide search for leaders to participate
in a highly lucrative program designed to create
lifetime residual wealth for 15 individuals . . .

Dear Colleague,

The lawyers have finally finished, the contracts have been signed, the money has been paid and the merger is complete. Biogime has just purchased the assets of the Diamond Falcon Corporation.

So this presents a lucrative opportunity for you . . .

But I'm getting ahead of myself. Let me fill you in with some of the important background information first. Biogime began as a retail and direct sales operation in 1986. We are owned by Entourage International, a multi-million dollar corporation with licensee operations in 11 countries. Although we recently unveiled a complete nutritional line, we are best known for our world-class skin care line. In 1994, we made a decision to transform Biogime into a network marketing company. This would allow us to attract the kind of leaders we were looking for and allow them to earn what they are really worth.

So we set out to build the country's best network marketing company . . .

One that someone like you would be proud to work with. As a former Divisional Manager with Watkins, I brought the experience of turning a direct sales company into a network marketing one. Biogime had Glen Rawlins & Damien Kuolt design the most "user friendly" compensation plan in the industry – one you can profit from in 11 ways. We retained Creative Design Concepts from Milwaukee, Wisconsin to oversee the creation of stunning collateral materials – materials you would be proud to work with. The company brought in Julie Martin to be president and CEO because of her strong management and financial background. And finally we struck an agreement with MLM guru Randy Gage to oversee the design and implementation of a complete, step-by-step, duplicatable system for distributors to follow. So this "dream team" of talent started to create the ultimate network marketing opportunity.

We set up the complete system and worked out the bugs. We developed some of the most duplicatable sponsoring materials in the industry. Training programs were designed and we did an informal kick-off last September in Las Vegas.

Everything was moving smoothly until recently . . .

That's when the opportunity arose to purchase Diamond Falcon. DF is the maker of SWIPE, the amazing product that swept the industry almost 30 years ago. This product line is producing sales in the tens of millions of dollars around the world.

Thus the opportunity for you that I spoke about earlier . . .

We consolidated the two companies and are now ready to launch the new Biogime across the country. We are gong to select 15 leaders to spearhead this drive. The people selected have the opportunity to reach levels of success most people only dream about. These 15 people will live their dreams. They will receive direct company sponsorship and business building support from Randy, myself and the entire corporate staff.

I'm inviting you to apply for one of these 15 positions.

We're looking for people who are serious about success. Previous experience is not as important as attitude. If you believe in network marketing and are committed to success, you could be the person we're looking for.

However, it is only fair to warn you . . .

If you're an MLM junkie looking for someone to build your group for you or think you can get rich just by mailing postcards, please don't respond. There are a lot of potential deals for you, ours is not one of them.

On the other hand, if you're honest, hard working, coachable and willing to follow a step-by-step system, I encourage you to apply immediately. *To do so, call me direct at (713) 827-1972 from 9 am to 4 pm Central time, or you may leave a message on my voice mail at 800-673-1944.* We'll chat a little and see if you qualify to be one of our 15 leaders. I'm looking forward to hearing from you.

Best regards,

Beth Royall

Beth Royall
National Marketing Director

P.S. We will select 15 people *only* for this lucrative situation. So I recommend that you call me immediately if you believe you are qualified.

CLARENCE LARK, JR.
President & Business Manager

A special message for Local 390 members . . .

Dear Member,

Enclosed you'll find an article about Dr. Bob Hochstein who has been serving our local for several years. Please take a few minutes to look it over. You may be suffering from conditions that can be corrected.

And as a member of Local 390, Dr. Hochstein is offering you a free, no obligation examination and consultation. If you are experiencing pain of any kind, please schedule an appointment to see if you can be helped. It may be one of the most important calls you make.

Sincerely,

Clarence Lark Jr.
President and Business Manager

Freight Drivers, Warehousemen and Helpers
Local Union No. 390
AFFILIATED WITH
INTERNATIONAL BROTHERHOOD OF TEAMSTERS, CHAUFFEURS, WAREHOUSEMEN AND HELPERS OF AMERICA
SOUTHERN CONFERENCE OF TEAMSTERS   GEORGIA FLORIDA CONFERENCE OF TEAMSTERS
2940 N.W. 7TH STREET   MIAMI, FLORIDA 33125-4395   (305) 641-6256 and 493-0904

CLARENCE LARK, JR.   JOHN R. TAYLOR
President and Business Manager   Secretary Treasurer

THE M.D., CAT SCAN, NEUROLOGIST, MRI
AND PRESCRIPTIONS COULDN'T HELP ME . . .

Dear Local 390 Member,

A short while back I wrote you urging you to seek help from Chiropractic Physician Robert Hochstein if you or anyone in your family was in pain.

Little did I know that the person getting help would be me.

I suffered from excruciating headaches and neck pain, to the point of disrupting my sleeping for nine months. My family medical doctor tried many things – I went to a neurologist, got a CAT scan, an MRI, other tests, and took prescription drugs. These things brought me only limited relief. I was facing a chancy operation or a life of pain.

Until Delores Ates urged me to follow my own advice and see if Dr. Hochstein and chiropractic care could help me.

The results . . .

I got immediate relief of my headaches and the neck pain is better. I've discontinued the medication, and I'm able to sleep again. My posture is noticeably better, and I've even had relief from kidney and bladder problems.

And that's why I'm writing you again . . .

Dr. Hochstein has agreed to give <u>a complete consultation and examination, free of charge, to Local 390 members and their families</u>. To take advantage of this free offer and to schedule your free exam, call (305) 654-9797, let them know I sent you and tell them you are in the Local 390. The Chiropractic Care Center is located at 441 and County Line Road, minutes from anywhere. Please don't put up with symptoms or pain needlessly, like I did – go in and get your free examination.

To your good health,

Clarence Lark, J.

Clarence Lark
President & Business Manager

CLARENCE PITTMAN
President

A special message for Longshoremen members . . .

Dear Member,

Enclosed you'll find an article about Dr. Bob Hochstein who has been serving our Local for several years. Please take a few minutes to look it over. You may be suffering from conditions that can be corrected.

As a member of the Longshoremen, Dr. Hochstein is offering you a free, no obligation examination and consultation. If you are experiencing pain of any kind please schedule an appointment to see if you can be helped. This is good for your family members also. It may be one of the most important calls you make.

Sincerely,

Clarence Pittman

Clarence Pittman
President

P.S. Please know that Dr. Hochstein is an approved Humana PPO provider so your union insurance will apply. Dr. Hochstein also accepts automobile insurance and workers comp.

Dr. Robert Hochstein
Chiropractic Physician

A special note to my friends in Blue . . .

Dear PBA Member,

It was about 6:30 on a Saturday evening when the accident happened. The policeman's injuries were by no means life threatening, but he was in acute pain.

He arrived at the ER to find there were about 40 people in line in front of him. You would think a man in blue might be bumped to the front of the line, but it was not to be on this day. You can't really blame the hospital either – they had their hands full with gunshot wounds, stabbings, lawn-mower maimings and the usual Saturday night episodes.

In the meantime, however, our officer is still in intense pain. The ER staff appreciates his condition, but lets him know that he probably won't be taken care of for about 4 to 6 hours.

The goddess of fate had her eye on our officer. His partner was a patient of mine. And like all my patients, had my phone number at home.

Ninety minutes later our officer had been examined, X-rayed, received acute care, and a cervical collar and was resting at home already feeling better.

We don't get emergencies like this all the time at my office. In fact, most of the PBA members who come to me are a result of getting in and out of a patrol car 20 or 30 times a day with a bullet proof vest and a heavy gun belt on.

Either way, we take the best care possible of whoever comes to my office. I try hard to honor the oath I took when I graduated from Chiropractic College ". . . to stand ready at all times to serve my fellow man . . ." But I take extra special care of the men and women in blue . . . and their families. Because I know what you go through. And I appreciate it.

Which is the real purpose of my letter . . .

Because I have a very special offer for you. Please read the enclosed Special Report entitled "Stop the Pain." **If you or anyone in your family suffers from any of the 13 danger signs on page 3 – please call my office immediately.** At the back of the report you'll find a certificate good for a free no-obligation examination. It's my gift to you to show my appreciation of the PBA.

Please use the certificate so we can determine if chiropractic care can help you or your family. And if continuing care is needed, we accept most insurances, including auto accident, workman's compensation, HMOs and PPOs.

There is just no reason for you or your family members to be in pain. Call me at (305) 654-9797 if I can help in any way.

Warmly,

Robert Hochstein, D.C.

Robert Hochstein, D.C.

P.S.   The certificate for the free check-up is on page 7 of the Special Report. It's yours with my appreciation for the good work you do.

**An invitation to be one of only 8 people to participate in a lucrative new "pilot" program
I want to try out...**

Dear Colleague:

I just got off the phone with Dennis & Mella Shoebotham, our first Emerald Executives, and the top distributors in the Northwest. They've agreed to participate in a fascinating new program to take 8 people from Washington state and put them through the most intensive success programming ever conducted in Network Marketing.

That means you have an unprecedented income opportunity -- like none you've ever had the chance to cash in on.

It's something that's never been attempted before and frankly, I'm excited. Here's what we're looking to accomplish:

The 8 people selected will be personally sponsored by Dennis & Mella (you may remember them from the profile about them in Upline Magazine). Then these 8 people will go through our Fast Track Mentor Program -- which has the potential to skyrocket your income in a matter of months.

In this program, the 8 people selected will get personal guidance, training, coaching, help with presentations, camera ready ads, sample sponsoring letters, 3-way calls, special business building materials and just overall assistance and wisdom from Dennis, Mella and the Company.

I will also personally be working with the 8 people selected by Dennis & Mella. If you qualify, you'll get guidance from the #1 distributorship in the country, plus all the resources of my office at your disposal. In fact, I'll be flying to Seattle to work with you on February 5th.

Why would we go to such great lengths to make you successful? Two reasons really.

First, it's just good business. When we have lots of distributors making money - WE make money. Simple economics.

Second, for research purposes. I'm betting that this Fast Track Mentor Program can take someone with little or no networking experience, but a real desire to make it - and turn them into a networking superstar. This type of training has never been attempted before - New Resolution is the first company to do this.

Here's what you get if you qualify:

Personal sponsorship by Dennis & Mella, our #1 distributorship in the country. A direct line to me at company headquarters in Milwaukee. One of 8 slots in the mentor program to follow the training system developed exclusively for NRI by Networking Guru Randy Gage. In other words, the opportunity to absolutely explode your earnings potential.

And, if you're not familiar with New Resolution, let me bring you up to date. We stunned the industry by picking up the exclusive, worldwide rights to Pep-A-Trim. Our free car program, Founder's Club, and profit sharing fund make NRI the most lucrative plan you can work with. Our latest product innovation, 2F-Plus, is destined to be the #1 sizzle product of 1994. And now this New Mentor Program can put _you_ in the driver's seat.

I'm writing to invite you to be one of the 8 people selected.

This invitation is severely limited. We will select 8 people only, 9 is too many. Quite frankly, the people we choose for this program have the potential to reach levels of success few ever experience. If this works as well as I think it can, we will use these 8 people for similar programs in other states.

This is not a sales letter. It's merely a formal announcement for a maximum of 8 people who are coachable, persistent and serious about making money.

How do you find out if you're qualified?

If you procrastinate, are ego driven or are unwilling to act on profitable ideas - please don't waste your time or mine. If, on the other hand, you are coachable, willing to follow a step-by-step system and are highly motivated towards success -- please call Dennis & Mella at (206) 935-8679 right now.

They'll ask a few questions, answer some of yours and let you know if you're qualified for the Fast Track Mentor Program. I do hope we'll be working together.

Warmly,

James C. Hoffman

Jim Hoffman
Vice President, Distributor Service

P.S. A program like this has never been done before. A distributor with this much help, guidance, training and nurturing can achieve massive success. But, remember, there are 8 openings only - so I urge you to call immediately if you're at all qualified.

Randy Gage

**A special invitation for students of truth to arise and claim
your inheritance and experience the divine joy of living total truth . . .**

Dear Friend of Unity,

Emilie Cady tells us "every right thought we think, our every unselfish word or action, is bound by immutable laws to be fraught with good results." Put in simpler terms: You can't outgive God.

But as we journey the path of light, it's important that we focus not on the results of the walk, as these things are the "loaves and fishes." Rather, we must seek to <u>become</u> truth conscious – to be love, wisdom and life – and let the results come forth through Divine Destiny.

When we are one with our destiny – truth radiates from us and accomplishes God's work. And that's why I'm writing to you.

I have never written a letter like this before. I doubt I'll ever write another like it again. *But a situation (and thus an opportunity) has arisen that offers you a chance to become truth, love and wisdom, if that is what you are seeking.*

But I'm getting a little ahead of myself. First, let me bring you up to date on the state of your church.

1993 was a year of challenge, growth and adventure. As we begin 1994, we are at a crossroads. The need for the Unity message has never been greater both in Miami and around the world. The church is presented daily with opportunities to serve. And thankfully, as I announced to resounding applause a few weeks ago . . .

UNITY ON THE BAY IS BACK!

Sunday attendance is getting stronger and stronger. Father Fred and the other new additions to the choir have brought it to levels of excellence seldom seen. Some days the music and joy seem to emanate from them with enough force to be felt for hundreds of miles. Our Spanish Ministry takes place every Sunday and is spreading light to our Latin brothers and sisters. We've begun a Gay and Lesbian Support Group to help them seek truth and affirm that they are God's children too.

A Course In Miracles continues to reach more and more people through the facilitation of Jay Burke. The Christmas Eve fellowship, Carol Pratt's "Spicy Mix" and the New Year's Eve program attracted more people to our church (downtown after dark) than we've seen in about 10 years!

Opportunities for spiritual, physical; and mental development abound. Virtually every day of the week has a class to offer you. From Yoga to the 12 Steps Are For Everyone . . . from spiritual economics to dance . . . from lessons in Truth to the 4T Prosperity program. We are truly becoming our mission as a radiating center of light, love, peace and truth.

It's a far cry from close to a decade ago when the mother church was ready to write off this location as a victim of crack, crime and changing demographics. That was 10 years ago, but it seems like a hundred. The church today is so strong, has so much potential for good, it's difficult to envision just where we came from.

But there's a very earthbound and very real reminder of those years . . .

It comes in the form of a balloon payment on our mortgage and a roof that seems determined to let the heavens (and the rain) through to you.

Here's the story behind the story.

About the time when the church was ready to close and sell off the land, a fellow named Bill Cameron was experiencing what Eric Butterworth calls Divine Dissatisfaction. Bill was the senior minister at the Mother Church in Missouri. He was at the pinnacle of a long Unity career, but felt there should be more. He heard about the impending demise of Miami Unity on the Bay and felt led to resign from the Mother Church. He packed up, moved to Miami and took over Unity on the Bay.

What he found wouldn't make the average person feel very spiritual . . .

Sunday attendance was almost nonexistent. There were no classes to speak of – no one would come near the place at night. Carpets were ripped and threadbare, paint was peeling off the walls, many things were broken. The building wasn't recognizable as a church. Break-ins took place as many as 3 times a week. Bill sometimes took to sleeping over in the church with a baseball bat. Probably the first definitive moment came after a tremendous rain storm.

The roof had more holes than Swiss cheese, water was pouring in everywhere. A contractor was brought in to survey the interior damage, and he had some chilling news.

"You see that stuff hanging out of the ceiling tiles," he said. "that's asbestos."

One hundred thirty thousand dollars was needed to get it out. Somehow, love, light and good overcame the obstacles and the money was raised. But as part of that financing, a $40,000 balloon payment was placed on the mortgage

That balloon payment is due in two weeks.

And once again, love is responding. People are giving massages, baking food, making gingerbread houses, washing cars and just all around whatever they can to raise money. Many have committed $1,000 personally towards this "bust the balloon" effort. Over $23,000 has come in so far.

And time is running out . . .

If that weren't enough, this grand old building is facing a formidable foe – old age. Water pipes leak and break, wiring is obsolete, boards rot out. The copier is broken down again, and we need a FAX machine. These are occurrences to be expected at a church this age, and somehow we deal with them.

But the big problem now is our roof. It's been patched over so many times it's really beyond repair. Initial estimates put the replacement cost at $40,000.

We have reached the defining turning point . . .

For the good work this church does to continue, we need your help. You and the entire Unity family. From the people who come to the Course in Miracles . . . to anyone ever assisted by the counseling and support groups . . . from those who subscribe to the tape ministry . . . to those who found inner peace here one Sunday, or every week.

So I've been asked by my fellow Board of Directors members to get the message out to everyone who has ever found their spiritual needs met by Unity on the Bay.

Thus, the special opportunity for those seeking truth I spoke of earlier.

If you are seeking the path of spiritual light, this challenge offers you the chance to practice the principles Unity teaches – to become Love. Because only love, the Christ in You, can make this situation work.

We need about $65,000 to pay off this impending balloon payment and replace the roof properly. We only have about 1,000 people on the mailing list. Of those, many are visitors who stopped by once and didn't return. Many others have moved away. Of those who still attend regularly, many are unemployed or underemployed.

But I'm reminded of the story in the early days of Unity. A deputy from the sheriff's department showed up to repossess a printing press on which the payments were overdue. Charles Fillmore calmly told the officer to do whatever was necessary and have no worries, because he had a rich heavenly Father who would supply all needs. The deputy left and the printing press stayed.

So regardless of surface odds, I'm betting on Unity. This church has helped so many people over the years, created so much love – that love will overcome.

I look upon our challenge the same way Robert Schuler looked at building the Crystal Cathedral. It's quite simple actually. One person on the spiritual path could give $65,000. Or two could give $32,500 each. Ten people could make a love offering of $6,500 or 65 people could give $1,000 each. The possibilities are endless - even $5 helps.

If you're thinking of giving the $65,000, but wondering what we would do with the extra money that others give – trust me when I tell you that this won't be a problem. There are conferences we'd like to send the Youth of Unity (YOU) to, other outreach programs we'd like to fund, and we still need another coat of paint. Maybe we'll have enough left over to buy a FAX machine.

Emerson calls the law of compensation the "Law of Laws." Catherine Ponder thinks of it as a basic law of radiation and attraction. Course in Miracles and Unity thinking are that of you reap what you sow.

Charles Fillmore sent shock waves through the religious establishment when he declared, "It is a sin to be poor!" Unity was founded on the belief that when we become one with God consciousness – the entire universe flows into us with abundance of life, substance and prosperity.

I guess what I am saying is that what happens around you or to you is irrelevant – it is what happens in you that really counts. And I guess I'm also saying that this financial challenge can be the chance to begin or expand a change in you. A chance to claim your inheritance and experience total truth.

I have little else to tell you except that I'm sure you would want to know about this situation so you could take the action that is right for you. And remind you that the balloon payment is due March 15th, and the rainy season is rapidly approaching.

I've enclosed an envelope and reply card in the event that you feel led to participate. I realize that some of you may wish to contribute with a credit card so you may pay in affordable monthly payments, so we've made provisions on the reply card for that.

The entire board of directors joins me in thanking you for your love and support. Like you, we celebrate this opportunity to share Love and look forward to a 1994 of following a divinely directed path.

Peace and Blessings,

Randy Gage

Randy Gage
Vice President, Board of Directors

P.S. We are at the dawn of our turning point at Unity on the Bay. At this time of great challenge and thus great opportunity, it would serve us well to remember the words of Charles Fillmore in his call for a new age of man.

"In the new era now at it's dawn, we shall have a spirit of prosperity. The principle of the universal substance will be known and acted upon, and there will be no place for lack. Supply will be more equalized. There will not be millions of bushels of wheat stored in musty warehouses while people go hungry. There will be no overproduc-tion or underconsump-tion or other inequities of supply, for God's substance will be recognized and used by all people. Men will not pile up fortunes one day and use them the next, for they will not fear the integrity of their neighbors. Is this an impractical Utopia? The answer depends on you."

NOTES

NOTES

NOTES

NOTES

Massive Marketing By Mail

Probably the most intriguing possibility for people who want to build out their warm market is building by mail. People are fascinated with the prospect of mailing out thousands of letters and sponsoring massive numbers of people. This is probably the least duplicatable method to build of all possibilities. The primary reason for this, believe it or not, comes from the success you can have mailing.

It is possible to sponsor 25 or 30 business-builders a month with a successful mail campaign. Realistically, how can you really work with that many people? To spend one night a week with each person, teach them the standard presentation, do a "get-started" training, etc. is simply not possible. By its very nature, building by mail is inherently a survival-of-the fittest numbers game.

The other things that make building by mail unduplicatable are the high costs (for printing and postage), and the high-level skill set necessary to do direct mail successfully. To be effective in the mail requires an extensive knowledge of copywriting, postal practices and list selection.

As with the other strategies that are not very duplicatable - the less the average distributor has to do, the better. If the company or organization provides camera-ready letters, selects mailing lists and trains on how to handle responses, so much the better.

The other variable to keep in mind while designing any mail campaign simply is knowing what you want to accomplish with the campaign. Sounds easy, but few people think this out.

There are four primary scenarios:

Scenario one is the most common. This entails mailing out cheap post-cards or a cheap, low-quality tape in mass quantities hoping to sign up prospects in one swoop.

While this is the most prevalent technique - it is also the least effective. The kind of people who join a program because it's cheap ("no sign-up fee"), easy ("get rich just by mailing postcards") are not the type who build large networks. Likewise, the dimwitted folks who are so influenced by a tape claiming miracle products that bring dead doctors back to life. They will be just as easily influenced by the next tape they get a week or two later.

Scenario number two entails using a two-step or three-step by mail process - usually screening the prospect by requiring him to send a nominal amount of money to receive the information. These types of campaigns pull much less response percentage-wise, but they bring you much more qualified prospects, which usually translates into a higher conversion ratio to distributors.

This sequence follows the traditional sponsoring process - information presented in stages, each getting more in-depth - but it's done by mail rather than in person. Obviously, it's not as duplicatable as doing it in person and it takes longer, but it can work.

The third scenario is the one that seems to work best for the most people. In this strategy, an initial mailing is done, usually asking for a modest deposit toward the cost of the materials. Once the materials are sent to the prospect, the distributor follows up by phone several days later. The initial materials sent are usually some kind of pre-approach packet and a brief info pack on the opportunity.

Then, on this follow-up call, the distributor actually does a presentation on the phone. If the prospect is still interested and you believe she's qualified - you would then send out the next packet of information (usually by some form of expedited delivery) and again follow-up by phone, maybe several times. After a sequence of prolonged phone contacts like this - bonds develop and quite often lead to a relationship. I did quite a bit of this kind of sponsoring. I developed relationships with many people where I felt like I'd known them for years - although we had never met in person.

The fourth scenario is the most unduplicatable of all. As far as I know, I'm the only person who has ever pulled it off successfully. This was done to launch a company when there were no experienced corporate distributors to work with anyone who might respond.

We didn't have the marketing materials yet, but had about a thousand leads in response to an article that had run in one of the industry trade publications. What I tried to do was write a long-copy letter that would get people to sign up as distributors, buy an introductory pack of products and put down a credit card number for a monthly autoship - all without even seeing a brochure or speaking to a live person. Obviously I had lost touch of my faculties and it's a good thing too, because - it worked! On the following pages, I've included the actual package I mailed on the following pages, along with some of the other successful mailings I've designed.

The rules of copywriting we looked at in the earlier segment are very much in play here. Write good copy and it can make you wealthy. Write feature-centered, boring copy and it really is possible to send out 10,000 letters and not get a single response. The other area you must be proficient in is the mechanics of mailing (i.e., tracking response rates, selecting lists, etc.), which is what we'll look at in the next segment ....

9250 Rumsey Road, Suite 100, Columbia, MD 21045
(410) 715-9911   FAX: (410) 715-9922

Bernaldo J. Dancel
Chief Executive Officer

September 21, 1995

The letter you've been waiting weeks for...

Dear Colleague:

First off, let me apologize for the delay. I know it's been some time since you read the FREENET profile and called for information.

Although we knew the story was going to run, we had no idea it was going to appear so early. Compounding matters, from what we can tell, we may have received the largest response to a MLM story ever. I'm told a typical story might generate 150 to 200 inquiries. We received 117 calls the first day! The response rate is nearly a thousand and I have 2 employees working solely on getting the messages and calling back for address information.

We don't even launch until October 1st!

Which presents me with quite a dilemma. Our distributor kit and presentation materials won't be done till then, yet I have a thousand serious potential business builders like you, who want to know more. NOW.

Thus the purpose of my letter...

I've decided to explain the entire concept to you - and let you decide what's best for you. If you see enough to make a decision - send in the applications and we'll lock you into place with a direct sponsorship for October 1st. If you're intrigued by the concept, but not quite ready to decide - let me know that too, and we will have a distributor get back to you when the materials are available at the start of October. You be the judge.

Anyway, here's what I can tell you right now...

We have a program unlike anything else in the industry. There's a dozen ways for you to earn, and we offer benefits like group health insurance and a 401K retirement plan. I believe FREENET gives you the best value for your money in the industry and we're developing a first class, professional step-by-step duplicatable system for you to follow. Simply put, we're creating an environment that will allow you to build at your optimum speed, with support materials you'll be proud to use. Here's how it all came about:

About 5 years ago, I founded a non-profit credit counseling service. My goal was to help people who were over-extended on their credit cards and other debt obligations. As a non-profit organization, we could get interest rates lowered, late charges waived, accounts re-aged to current status and other things creditors might not do for you as an individual. It began on my kitchen table...

And soon took over my basement. And then a bigger basement in my next house. Which forced me to re-locate to a large office with 10 employees. Last year I went to 30 employees. I'm now moving to bigger offices in the best office building in Columbia, and my little "kitchen table" association has 85 employees and will do over 5 million dollars this year. I was selected as an Inc. Magazine Entrepreneur of the year finalist, and people come from around the world to see how I accomplished all this in only a few years.

But, I wasn't satisfied...

You see, although we are growing by leaps and bounds, I knew there were millions of people with credit problems that we hadn't reached yet.

I began to explore the possibility of network marketing. Having watched the industry for a number of years, I knew the powerful potential of this emerging business megatrend. I began a search for the person who could take my concept and marry it to the network marketing opportunities. One name kept coming up...

A reclusive marketing genius who lives on a little island between Miami and Miami Beach. He wears an earring, works in blue jeans and tennies (although he's partial to Armani suits) and won't even take a client without forty grand up front, five figure monthly retainer fees and a percentage of the profits. He's a high school drop-out who became a self made millionaire. His name is Randy Gage.

I called Randy and discussed what I had. He was intrigued enough to suggest I fly down to see him. I laid bare the entire concept that I envisioned. He told me that credit counseling service could be the hottest product in the industry – but the concept alone wouldn't fly. Too limiting, he said. While 40% or 50% of Americans need my service, that left half who didn't. Not a big enough universe to start a network marketing company. "However" he said...

"What about if you put the credit counseling together with other worthwhile financial discounts, services and opportunities? Kind of a 'Merrill Lynch for Joe Lunchbucket'."

"Make something for the average guy" he mused. "Something for the guy or gal who doesn't have stock brokers, financial planners and a personal relationship with the bank president."

"Group insurance. Benefits package. Discount long distance service. Travel discounts. Financial planning assistance. Retirement plan. Take all that and more - and put it together with the credit counseling. Then you've got the hottest concept to hit MLM in 20 years."

Instinctively, I knew he was right...

But I wanted to be sure. I took about a week, spoke to my board members and asked around to everyone I knew. The responses were quite telling...

One of my highly respected Board Members, Dr. Gene Sambataro, immediately committed to coming in as a partner and executive. The other people I talked to - both those experienced in MLM, and those who had never been involved - said the same thing:

"When can I sign up?"

We formed a company, inked a deal with Randy and set out to put together the ideal company. That was almost a year ago. Which leads me up to where we are today. And your interest in FREENET...

2

As I told you, we don't officially launch till October and won't have the complete duplicatable system in place until then. *But you're looking for something right now...*

So let me explain the plan to you and you can decide what to do next.

We've put together two very special options in the product department - the Gold Plus Plan and Platinum Elite Plan. Let's look at them.

The Gold Plus Plan offers you the very real chance to save thousands of dollars annually on a host of products and services. You also have the potential to earn thousands more by retailing individual parts of the plan or offering the whole package.

The first portion of the plan is the financial services. Probably the best place for you to start is with a Personal Financial Profile. As a Gold Plan Member, you'll get this at the wholesale price. This is a customized analysis of what you spend on clothes, rent or mortgage, food, entertainment - virtually every area of your budget. You'll be able to compare your costs with the normal average costs for your area to see where you can save money.

Another important segment of the financial services is the credit counseling. Here's how it works:

You or someone you know may be in debt beyond their ability to manage. If so, we will assign your account to a credit counselor with the non-profit association. They will immediately step in with your creditors and work to lower your monthly payments if necessary; get late fees waived; reduce your interest rate, and get your accounts re-aged to current status. You'll make just one lump sum payment to the organization and they will handle all of your individual bills. Once one account is paid off, they will increase the amounts to your remaining creditors and keep repeating this process until you are debt free. There's never been anything like this in MLM before. Yet this is just one small part of the Gold Plan.

Other parts of the financial portions of the Gold Plan include savings on home mortgages, a mortgage acceleration program (that can save you tens of thousands of dollars in interest costs), and even mortgage foreclosure consulting for people in danger of losing their house. There's also insurance services, secured credit cards and a tax audit hotline. This entire financial services package is just one forth of the Gold Plan.

The second part of the plan is the Consumer Benefit Package. This is the part that saves you money - lots of it. You get over $500 worth of grocery coupons - on the products you select - each year. Use them at a store that doubles or triples coupons and now you're talking serious money. In addition, you'll get special offers, discounts and savings on vision services, flower delivery, hearing aids, prescription drugs, moving services, medical supplies, restaurants, movies, car repair and more. *Tens of thousands of people across America joined programs like Fund America and CBI just to get this kind of benefits package. Yet it's just a small part of the FREENET Gold Plan.*

In addition, you can sign up for the FREENET long distance phone service, which gives you deep discounts on your phone bill. While many people are paying 20¢ a minute you'll be getting rates of 13.9¢ daytime and 11.9¢ night-time. Your calls will go through a state-of-the-art fiber optic network, with 1 plus outbound, 800 inbound services, discount calling cards and debit calling cards also available. *Thousands of people have joined network marketing companies that market only long distance service. With FREENET, this is just a fraction of the Gold Plan.*

The third component of the Gold Plan is the travel consultant program. Your Gold Plan membership automatically enrolls you as an authorized travel consultant. This means you get a rebate on your personal travel and a commission on any travel you sell to others. You also get the chance to go on familiarization

3

(FAM) trips sponsored by cruise companies and resorts at ridiculously low prices. If you can travel on short notice, you can participate in special "fire sale" offers on cruises or tours that may have a few spaces remaining. Anytime you travel you'll enjoy travel agent rates on hotels, rental cars, and tours. Many times you also receive extra perks, service and upgrades. It's not unusual for airlines to bump you to first class, and hotels to move you to the concierge floor due to the fact that you are an outside travel consultant that can send them additional business.

Make no mistake - this is not a timeshare or travel club with limited choices and tons of "fine print." As an actual authorized travel consultant, you'll know exactly what commission you receive on each service you book and you can go anywhere, anytime on any airline, cruise ship or train, and stay at any hotel and resort you want.

You'll especially like the final section of the Gold Plan. With it, you receive a paid membership in Entrepreneurs Alliance International (EAI). EAI will help you slash business costs while you also learn skills to help you grow your business.

Because EAI is a non-profit association - it can negotiate extra services, discounts and savings that you can't get by yourself. Simply show your EAI membership card and qualify for special savings and offers. Here's a small sample of some of the benefits you get immediately as a EAI member:

· Overnight delivery from Airborne Express for only $8.75 or $9.25,

· Save up to 50% off List Price on over 10,000 items from Boise Cascade office products,

· Save 10% to 15% off Moore business forms, envelopes, mailers, presentation folders and computer paper,

· 10% discount on copyright or trademark services from Stanley Lewis Legal Services,

· Low cost Term Life, Disability and Office Overhead Insurance,

· Take 10% off weekly car rentals from HERTZ and AVIS,

· 15% savings on Intuit Software for business owners,

· 10% off graphic design and printing from P & G Printing,

· Much, much more.

EAI also helps you learn marketing strategies to help you build your business faster. Each month you'll receive a copy of Free Enterprise Journal, the magazine exclusively for EAI members, packed with money making information.

Even better, you'll attend special Entrepreneur Alliance training seminars at deep discounts. The first two "Marketing Your Business" seminars, presented by some of the world's savviest marketers, are already set for Florida and California this fall. Other areas are scheduled for the spring. In addition, you'll be qualified to attend the annual EAI convention at member prices. This 3 day event is the ultimate chance to network, make contacts and learn from the world's top entrepreneurs.

4

There's yet more: You'll buy at wholesale price from the EAI Money Making Catalog. You'll save money on MLM training tools from Randy Gage, peak performance resources from Tony Robbins and Stephan Covey, sales building tapes from Dale Ledbetter and many other profit producing resources. And remember, this Entrepreneur's Alliance International membership is included at no cost in your Gold Plus Plan.

You probably expect all this to cost hundreds of dollars a month, since just one membership can save you thousands and thousands of dollars annually. Here's the amazing part: the Gold Plan membership sells for just $55 a month retail. As a FREENET distributor, you'll pay only $40 a month!

We haven't even talked about the Platinum Elite option yet...

This plan gives you everything that is included in the Gold Plan, plus the following:

· Personal Lease - a program that gives you special rates and assistance on automobile leasing.

· You get wholesale pricing on Financial Planning Services with 4 different modules available.

· Complimentary DRIVERS ONE card - which gets you free travel planning, roadside assistance, towing and a host of other car benefits,

· Complimentary subscription to Dale Ledbetter & Randy Gage's Sales & Marketing Success - Letter,

· The opportunity to join the FREENET Group Health Insurance Plan - premier protection at affordable prices,

· Your chance to participate in the 401K retirement plan with matching contributions from FREENET for directors and above,

· Other services, soon to come.

The retail cost for the Platinum Elite program is only $99 a month and your distributor cost is only $80. **Please pay very close attention to the next two paragraphs...**

Purchase the Gold Plan and your personal volume (PV) is $40 a month. Sign up for the Platinum Elite plan and your PV is $80 a month. *Sign up a retail customer for Gold - get $15 retail profit and $40 more personal volume - every month. Sign up a retail Platinum customer - get $19 retail profit and $80 additional personal volume - every month.*

You can also sell many individual components of either plan for retail profit! The Personal Financial Profiles, the Mortgage Acceleration Program, Mortgage Foreclosure Consulting, Discount Long Distance Service and Financial Planning Modules to name a few. Some services like the credit counseling and long distance service pay a percentage of sales back as PV to you each month. Every time you sell a Gold or Platinum Plan retail, it counts towards your personal volume. Every time someone in your group sells either plan retail, it counts toward your group volume. DO YOU HAVE ANY IDEA WHAT KIND OF AVERAGE VOLUMES THIS WILL PRODUCE FOR YOU TO GET BONUS CHECKS ON? DO YOU HAVE ANY IDEA?

As if that weren't enough, can you imagine the deliciously outrageous possibilities were you or your people to get churches, schools and other organizations selling Gold or Platinum Plan memberships for fund raising?

5

While we're on the subject of deliciously outrageous incomes, let me tell you about the compensation plan. You'll find it's one of the most "user friendly" stair step breakaway plans in the industry. We created a plan that pays out big dollars to top producers, but wasn't balanced on the backs of the little guy. For instance, when you break off a new director - your group volume needed to qualify for override bonuses is reduced by half the next month, and one third the month following that. We've even included vacation months to attract the professionals who look to network marketing as a career. The plan is so lucrative there are 11 ways to earn:

    1) Retail Profits
    2) Personal Rebates
    3) Group Overrides
    4) Qualified Directors Bonuses
    5) Leadership Override Bonuses
    6) A Free Car Fund
    7) Ruby Bonuses
    8) Emerald Bonuses
    9) Diamond Bonuses
    10) Special bonus pool (Contests for cash & prizes, and a free trip fund)
    11) Matching payments for your 401K Plan Contributions

Here's what else you should know...

There's a twelfth way to earn...one you won't find listed in the compensation plan. The Founders Club Here's how it works:

    •Qualify as an Emerald or Diamond Director within the first two years of FREENET operation - you're in the Founders Club. Once you're in - stay qualified as an Emerald or Diamond and you're vested for life. Once the two years qualifying time is up - no one else can join the club. One half of one percent of the entire company's sales volume goes into this fund. Once you're in you're in - once it's closed, no one else can get in. It wouldn't be an exaggeration, and it wouldn't be hype, to say the Founders Club has the potential to set you up for life. Really.

Of course, all this is dependent on you and your people having the materials and training you need to do this right. Here's where Randy Gage comes into the picture. He's created a complete, step-by-step, duplicatable system that anyone (sales type or non sales type, college educated or high-school drop-out), can follow. As a distributor you'll have an exact blueprint for success to follow. You'll know exactly what material to give a prospect at Step One, what to use for Step Two, for Step Three and every step on the prospecting - then sponsoring - then training process.

More importantly - every distributor you sponsor can simply, easily and faithfully follow the same exact process - the one and only criteria for true walk-away, residual lifetime income.

The other thing I insisted on was the quality of the support materials. I am consistently amazed at the junk I receive in the mail on a daily basis. Typo-filled brochures, homemade flyers, fuzzy copies and 10th generation knock off tapes. We're spending a fortune on producing support materials for you that:
    · Enhance the image of the industry;
    · You'll be proud to use;
    · Really Work!

6

Wait till October and you'll see what I mean. I'll stack the FREENET materials against anyone's. Even decade-old. billion-dollar companies. They're that good.

What else do you have to know?

One small thing, but it's quite important. I can't quite think of a polite way to say this, so let me be brutally honest: **If you're a freeloader or MLM junkie - we don't want you.** We have put together what is arguably the most lucrative, potentially powerful program in Network Marketing today. But it only works if you do.

If you're working other programs and want FREENET to compliment or supplement your portfolio - STAY AWAY. In the history of MLM, no one has ever built two or more programs to success levels at the same time. Never. I have no time to waste with delusional wannabes. Likewise for people who are looking for the deals where they "build your downlines for you" or you "get rich just by mailing postcards." If this is you, please throw this letter away right now. I don't need your money and you wouldn't fit in.

Now, assuming you're not in one of those two groups, how do you determine if FREENET is the right program for you? Ask yourself these four questions:

    1)   Does the product/service line sound like something you would use personally and enthusiastically recommend?

    2)   Are you self-motivated, committed to success and willing to work 7 to 10 hours a week with a personal commitment to do your best for a one year trial period?

    3)   Are you coachable, willing to follow a duplicatable system, and also understand how important that is to the long term success of you and your people?

    4)   Are you tired of hearing about MLM history and ready to make some?

If you answered YES to all four questions, then it's highly likely that you have found the program of your destiny - the one you are truly meant to do. Please check the appropriate box on the following page and return it with the proper applications in the enclosed envelope. Or better yet, FAX them to me at (800) 660-9849.

That's about all I have to tell you about this fascinating program, other than to say that I believe we've created the ideal MLM concept - and I hope you'll be a part of it.

To your best success,

Bernaldo J. Dancel

P.S. Needless to say, the premise of this letter is unorthodox at the very least. But like you, I was once searching for the perfect opportunity. And if FREENET is as ideal for you as I believe it might be - I want you to have this information now, when you need it. I'm sure you understand.

7

Check Appropriate Box

☐   O.K. Bernie, you've got my interest, but I'm from the "show-me" state. Please have a distributor contact me after October 1st when your materials are all completed.

- -

(Return the "I Can Wait" form)

☐   Bernie, I can't wait. I have waited my whole life already for a program like this. I want in on the pre-launch stage for a head start. Please lock me in as a charter distributor. Here's my check for my membership and distributor kit which I'll receive in October. Please start the membership plan I've selected in October also.

I have enclosed:

1) The "I Can't Wait" and "Customer Agreement" forms

2) My check:

Distributor Kit$40.00
Membership $_____
Total $_____

- -

☐   I'm not interested in building a business at this time, but I want all the benefits and savings of being a retail customer. Please begin the plan I've selected beginning October 1st.

(Return the "Customer Agreement" form only)

8

HALL OF FAME

NRI Recruiting Letters

This was a series of letters that were used with slight variations in about 5 different states. They averaged a 2-3% response rate, depending on the region and timing, with approximately a 1/4 conversion ratio to distributors.

The letter you see was mailed to the Charles Possick Primo list and KAAS Publishing's MLM list. This is the draft copy as the final was not in my files.

The final three pages are the follow-up letter that was sent. Both mailings were sent in a #10 envelope with Jim's name, return address and the words, "Critically Important" above and slightly to the left of the mail panel. A blue rag content paper was used for the envelope and the letter.

The final copy of the first one was not in my files, so I have used the proof copy.

JAMES A. HOFFMAN
VICE PRESIDENT

An invitation to be one of only 12 people to receive a direct company sponsor ship and customized business building assistance from the corporate staff as part of a pilot program I want to try out...

Dear Friend:

I just got off the phone with NRI company president Penny Loppnow. She told me that my test program, "Operation Denver Storm", has been approved for immediate start-up. *That means you have an unprecedented income opportunity - - like none you have ever had the chance to cash in on.*

Just what is Operation Denver Storm?

It is a concept I have been kicking around for about 180 days. As you may have read, the 1st annual NRI company convention will be held in Denver on October 15 & 16. This has the makings of being the most powerful gathering ever held for distributors wanting to build huge organizations.

North America's #1 Networking Coach Randy Gage, will be unveiling the new business building materials he developed exclusively for NRI ... John Milton Fogg, Author of The Greatest Networker in the World will be the keynote speaker ... the new products that will set the pace for 1994 will be announced ... and much, much, more.

Because the convention will be held in Denver, we plan on conducting a massive statewide blitz for distributors who are serious about making money. We will be approaching all present and former network marketers in Colorado. We will show them the benefits of working a company that can provide sizzle products, the fairest compensation plan in the industry, on time bonus checks and company sponsored training.

I am writing to invite you to be one of the top leaders for this Colorado blitz

We will select 12 people TOPS to open the State. Those 12 leaders will be directly sponsored by the company. The corporate staff and I will personally be working with them, and they will benefit directly from the massive advertising campaign we will be conducting. Anyone responding after these initial twelve are selected will be placed in the organizations of these people.

Quite frankly, the people I choose for this program have the potential to reach levels of success few ever experience. If this works as well as I think it can, we will use these 12 leaders for similar programs in other states.

This is not a sales letter. It is merely a formal announcement and invitation for a *maximum of 12 people*, who are coachable, persistent and serious about making money.

<u>This invitation is severely restricted.</u>

It is only being extended to people who have proven their talents in the past and a very small group of others that I believe are capable of success provided they have a solid program to follow such as this one.

If you have been following publications like Money Makers Money and The Network Trainer - then you know NRI is positioned for massive momentum in 1994. Between the 3 current "sizzle" products that have everyone buzzing ... the new ones to be unveiled in Denver ... and the completely duplicatable system that ~~networking guru~~ Gage created for NRI - - It is highly likely we will set new records in the next 12 months. I sure hope you can be part of it.

In summary, here's what I'm offering you ...

The opportunity to be part of a breakthrough pilot program. Direct sponsorship and personal, customized support from the corporate office. Participation in the company sponsored advertising co-op and a chance to share in all the perks in the NRI compensation plan - profit sharing bonuses, travel awards, leadership bonuses and the free car program. <u>And more importantly</u>, a unique opportunity to qualify for the Founder's Club ... *which has the potential to set you up for life!*

However, I must fairly warn you ...

What I am offering you is not for everyone. It is for serious people who want to make serious money. We are looking for product centered people with integrity ... who are seeking financial independence and willing to do what it takes. Experience is really not as important to us as someone who is enthusiastic, teachable and willing to follow a system.

If you simply want to mail postcards, work several programs at once or are looking for a fast money game - - please do not bother to reply. We don't need your money and you wouldn't fit in.

If you qualify and you would like to be part of this fascinating pilot program, call me direct at (414) 646-2915 and we will supply you with complete details. Please do not wait and miss out - I am hoping to work with you.

Warmly,

~~Continued Success~~

James C. Hoffman

P.S.

If you are uncertain or uncomfortable with this offer, I recommend you do not respond. We have no desire or intent to persuade people who shouldn't be a part of this program to do so. People who understand and appreciate the significance of this opportunity are the only ones this program is intended for. ~~Thank You.~~

effort

project

I'm sure you under-stand.

NEW RESOLUTION INC

P.O Box 127

Delafield WI
53018 0127

N.R.I.

Aurora. Co. 0014-3343

Ref: Your application to be
one of the 12 leaders
selected for the Colorado
Blitz.

Dear ▮▮▮

    Thanks for your phone call, it was a pleasure to talk with
you. Your excitement about participating in "Operation Denver
Storm" is warranted.

    We will be selecting <u>only</u> 12 people to receive a direct
company sponsorship with customized business building
assistance from myself and the corporate staff. This will
include participation in company sponsored advertising co-op
and the chance to share in all the parts of the NRI
compensation plan - profit sharing bonuses. travel awards.
leadership bonuses and the free car program. Of course it goes
without saying that the 12 people we select have an inside
track to founder Club qualification ...*which has the potential to
set you up for life*.

And the big date is only weeks away!

    As I told you the first annual convention hits Denver on
October 15th and 16th. You could be on stage as one of the
emerging leaders. But you must act quickly!

    Please immediately review the material on NRI that I've
enclosed. There are 5 critical points to consider while you're
doing this...

1)   You will make what you're really worth! With the most innovative compensation plan in the industry. You get profit sharing bonuses, cash for free trips, leadership extras and you can even qualify for a free car.

2)   **You will be proud and feel secure working with NRI.** Bonus checks are always on time, first class promotional materials and timely deliveries provide you with the customer service you deserve!

3)   You will LOVE the products! Not because you buy them to get a check, but because their quality is superior, they're priced right and they work.

4)   Your organization (and thus, your profits) will **grow quicker with NRI.** Because we have invested in a proven duplicable system with effective support materials and company sponsored training nationwide. You get the security and residual/income that can only come from having a system provided by the company.

5)   **You still have time to qualify for the Founders Club.** Imagine what this could do for your life!

And as soon as you review this...

call me immediately at (414) 646-2915 and see if there are still positions available. If there is, we can discuss if you qualify, and if so, how we can get you started immediately. Because time is so short, be prepared to fax or overnight your application and first order in.

One last thing, it may be important...

As you know, the 12 people selected for this program have the potential to achieve levels of success few ever experience.

And because of that, I just wanted to reiterate what I mentioned in the last letter. If you're looking for a postcard scheme, money game or quick fix -- NRI is not the company for you.

If however, on the other hand... you're a product centered person with integrity - who is not afraid of success and the effort it requires - be sure and call me immediately so we can get to work.

Warmly,

James C. Hoffman
Vice President

P.S.   I have just learned that Dr. Michael Heigi will be speaking at the Denver convention! Dr. Heigi is one of the world's foremost experts in the fields of nutrition and supplement development. He's one of the pioneers in the research into the use of the aloe vera plant for nutritional and medicinal purposes. He will be sharing some of the background and inside information on his development of the Aloe-More and Renew-U products. Don't miss it!

HALL OF FAME

"Masked Man" Mailing

This piece was delicious! It once produced a 5% response on a cold, rented list. It was 2 color on 50 lb coated stock.

The concept was to bring guests to an opportunity meeting. It worked. However, it created logistical problems in handling so many unknown guests at an open meeting and corralling them into becoming distributors.

I don't know how or when - but somewhere, somehow, someday - the "masked man" will ride again...

WHO IS THIS MASKED MAN?

FIRST CLASS MAIL

GR&DI, Inc.
7501 East Treasure Dr.
Lobby Floor
North Bay Village, FL 33141

WHO IS THIS MASKED MAN?
And more importantly . . .

Can he help YOU make thousands
upon thousands of dollars?

See inside for details!

THIS MASKED MAN IS THE FOREMOST NETWORK MARKETER ALIVE TODAY.

Thousands of grateful distributors and clients owe their success to this man. Companies can pay as much as $20,000 a day for his time. He's generated millions & millions of dollars of sales. On a good day he rakes in more money than you may earn in a whole year.

AND HE WANTS

TO BE HIS NEXT PARTNER

Here's what the media says about our "Mystery Man":

". . . the highest paid, most sought after speaker / trainer / consultant in the industry."
Cutting Edge Opportunities

". . . the man America turns to for advice when they want to open a home based Network Marketing Business."
FTL Radio Network

"███████ █████ has helped thousands through his training seminars, tapes, videos and his ████████ █████ ████████"
Money Maker's Monthly

". . . one of Network Marketing's foremost trainers."
Upline

"████ is now a personal coach to thousands."
Opportunity Connection

". . . North America's #1 Networking Coach."
Profits Magazine

"His stable of admirers reads like a veritable who's who of the Industry . . . the definite 'how-to expert in the field."
FreEnterprise Magazine

He's become wealthy by helping people like you achieve their dreams in Network Marketing.

(See inside)

NOTES

NOTES

NOTES

Crafting Display Ads That Really Work

I must confess. Before I understood about having a duplicatable system - I did quite a bit with display ads. In fact, I get residual income to this day for ads I ran almost ten years ago. There is a trade-off, however. I don't see consistent growth in lines started by display ads like I see with warm market lines.

Quite simply - display ads are not completely unduplicatable, but they are less duplicatable than classifieds and much less so than warm market prospecting.

I find display ads work best when an organization head or the company provides completely designed ads, camera ready for the distributors. It also becomes more duplicatable when, let's say, six or eight distributors share the expense of a full-page ad and distribute the leads appropriately. This is preferable to one person paying big dollars for ads and working all the leads herself - or even worse - paying for the entire ad and giving the leads free to her organization. Doing this sets you up as the "hero" and sends the wrong message down the organization.

Increasing Display Ad Responses

■ Use a photo.

■ Use a graphic.

■ Include a coupon.

■ Use a toll-free number.

■ Add color (or delete color).

■ Use a compelling headline.

■ Run it consistently.

■ Ask for action.

■ Offer a FREE gift.

■ Offer a FREE booklet or brochure.

■ Offer a FREE estimate, consultation, evaluation, etc.

Most Common Display Advertising Mistakes

- You don't use a headline.

- You don't lead with the main benefit.

- You appeal to logic instead of emotion.

- Your copy is not "you"-oriented.

- You don't put benefits in the opening paragraph.

- Your message is not focused.

- You lie to readers.

- You don't give an incentive to act NOW.

- You mention price before benefits.

- You forget testimonials.

- You don't reverse the risk.

- You don't make it easy to buy.

- Your visuals don't have captions.

- You don't use photos or graphics.

- Your company logo is the prominent feature.

- You use too much reverse copy.

- Your layout is symmetrical.

- You don't key your ad.

- You use a P.O. box.

- You use an "artistic" font which is hard to read.

- You use too many different fonts.

Cell Tech

Money Maker's Monthly company of the Month
Over $150 Million In Last Year!
Networks Growing at 15% A Month!
Profiled In Success Magazine
Rated #1 By MLM Insider Magazine

The Super Blue Green™ product line developed and produced by Cell Tech, a solid, established 14 years old company, is gaining widespread recognition in the mass marketplace. Now is a first-rate time for you to start a Super Blue Green™ business. People are hearing about the products, yet market saturation is still many years away.

An incredibly successful, supportive and knowledgeable upline!

When you join the Super Health Network you'll have one of the most successful uplines in all of Cell Tech. You'll receive dynamic, personal training and support.

We provide you with strategies for:

-- Developing warm/cold markets.
-- Building distributor networks through health clubs, hair salons, church and civic groups and more.
-- Making the best use of cost effective marketing opportunities.

We help:

-- MLM professionals **grow large business builder downlines.** Have access to subscriber lists of **Success, Entrepreneur magazines** for direct mail prospecting.
-- Those with limited income reach their warm markets by sending out free tapes for you in your first three months.

We have tapes for specific "niche" markets: tapes by and for athletes, Evangelical Christians, Afro-Americans, Hispanic Americans. Also, tapes geared for those interested in the business opportunity, and for those most interested in the health benefits of the products. There are even tapes by veterinarians and animal trainers - on Cell Tech's wonderful animal algae.

We organize:

Large "cooperative" advertising in which you can share in the responses, but don't spend lots of money. We obtain mail/phone lists of persons looking for MLM business opportunities.

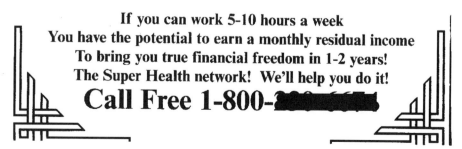

If you can work 5-10 hours a week
You have the potential to earn a monthly residual income
To bring you true financial freedom in 1-2 years!
The Super Health network! We'll help you do it!
Call Free 1-800-

JEWELS BY

PARK
LANE

CELEBRATING OVER 41 YEARS OF SUCCESS

THE OPPORTUNITY OF A LIFETIME

Control your schedule and your income.
The power for promotion is in your own hands.
Affiliate with people who are, positive, motivated, and supportive.

THE RIGHT PLACE!
- High fashion designer jewelry
- Enjoy recognition and awards
- Fabulous customer discounts
- Incredible hostess award program
- Fully guaranteed, high quality product

THE RIGHT TIME!
- Exciting travel trip contest to Jamaica, Cancun, & Hawaii
- Discover financial independence
- Exciting buying plan
- Start-Up bonus for qualified managers
- Variety of home accessory awards

THE RIGHT COMPANY!
- In-home / In-office sales
- Direct sales
- Catalog sales
- Phone-in / Fax orders
- High weekly profit checks
- Cash bonus incentives
- Dream vacations
- Diamonds, luxurious coats
- Car program

MAKE YOUR DREAMS
A REALITY WITH
JEWELS BY PARK LANE,
A COMPANY WITH
STABILITY
AND EXPERIENCE.

☎ For more information call ☎

1 - 800 - ●●●●●●●●●

SEEKING EXPERIENCED
DIRECT SALES LEADERS
FOR MAJOR FALL '96
EUROPEAN EXPANSION.
CALL TODAY!

QUALIFY FOR A MANAGEMENT SALES VOLUME BONUS FROM
$10,000 to $50,000

$10,000
Reward !

To the first person to show us a MLM pay plan or personal wealth generating system better than Linear Expansion™...

★ Only 3 personal Marketers needed for maximum payout!

★ Earn over $10,000 per month with only 100 active Marketers!

★ Unblockable, Unstoppable 35% Infinity Bonus with no cut-off ever!

★ 100% Matching Bonus on earnings of Personal Recruits!

★ No Group Volume requirements!

★ One-of-a-kind, cutting edge, exclusive products ("Quit for Life™" 100% Guaranteed, Original Stop Smoking Supplements.)

★ Massive National Co-Op Ad Campaign (share leads from this and other ads.)

★ Experienced "Dream Team" management.

★ Seven figure financial backing.

MLM just became obsolete! Once you've experienced the power of Interactive Marketing™ and the dynamics of the new, revolutionary, evolutionary Linear Expansion™ Pay Plan, you will never even consider another MLM company again! Earn at least 30 times more for the same effort than in any MLM program. We invite you to evaluate this truly exceptional opportunity for yourself — and position yourself as one of the key leaders in our company! Act now! **(Corporately Sponsored Ad)**

Every Marketer's Dream Come True!
For FREE Information Pack, call:

800-████████ **(24 hours)**

Your Prospectus Will Be Rushed to You, Today!

THE Art OF BETTER LIVING INC.

© copyright 1996 The Art of Better Living, Inc., Scottsdale, Arizona
Linear Expansion™, Interactive Marketing™ and Quit for Life™ are trademarks of The Art of Better Living, Inc.

From my "Hall of Fame":

This ad is a perfect example of what happens when you know the marginal net worth of a distributor to you.

It was run in the old "Opportunity Connection" magazine and produced quality distributors at a cost of about $45 each. That was about 4 years ago. Many of those distributors are still active today - producing tens of thousands of dollars of income for the principals involved.

10 REASONS
YOU NEED TO CALL NOW! ! !

#1) **You will catch Critical Mass.** This is the fastest growing Direct Sales/MLM company in America. (Adding 35,000+ monthly).

#2) **You will have one of the finest sponsorship lines in the industry.** 6 levels of six figure Power Players.

#3) **You will be proud and feel secure working with the company.** Six years steady, stable growth - listed in the Top 50 of the INC. 500.

#4) **You will LOVE the products!** Not because you buy them to get a check, but because you love them.

#5) **You will have a high Re-order ratio.** First, because the products are priced like REAL products that REAL people buy at REAL prices, and second because of the finest insurance/safety valve plan in the industry.

#6) **You will make what you're really worth!** With the most innovative 7 level marketing plan in the industry. One that rewards you for helping your people to be successful with healthy retail profits, new product introduction bonuses, organizational bonuses and executive incentives like a car fund.

#7) **You will be entering a proven, duplicatable SYSTEM.** First class professional Intro Kits, Lit Packs, sponsoring materials and company provided training.

#8) **Because if you don't call now - in 60 days someone will be calling you!**

#9) **Because you're tired of getting in on the ground floor - only to find out there's a basement!**

#10) Because the suspense is killing you!

1 (

This is the "10 Reasons" Ad, dusted off and cleaned up for 1995. It was run as a double truck in order to hold the centerfold section of "The Network Trainer." It could still be quite effective as a single page ad.

11 REASONS YOU NEED TO CALL NOW!!!

1 You can drive a new car. Thanks to the most lucrative car program in the entire networking industry, qualifying is easy. Our company has the largest luxury car fleet in the world. We've awarded over 30,000 (no this is not a typo) bonus cars – we'd love nothing better than for you to be driving one.

3 You'll build your business with confidence and security. This company has been in business for the last 38 years – and it will be here for the next 38. We're well funded, backed by a multi-billion dollar corporation, and we'll do over $600 million this year alone. You'll get the security of building a business you can leave to your grandchildren.

5 You'll join at the very start of the exponential growth explosion! Because this is a $600 million company that has been steadily expanding since the 1950s – but never hit critical mass. This "undiscovered jewel" has just been "discovered" by arguably the #1 network marketer in America. And he (or she) has joined the program with the intention of introducing it to the industry (with ads like this) and creating the momentum that will take the company to over the billion dollar mark within two years. This person is looking for 15 front line people to ride this wave to the top. You could be one of the 15 people selected if you hurry.

7 You'll have consistent income. Because you'll have the highest monthly consumption and re-order rate you've ever experienced. Not only are these products superior, but they are priced like REAL products that REAL people buy at REAL prices. Also because there are no buy-ins, front loading or any of the other nonsense.

2 You'll enjoy the pride of working with a first class company. You'll take pride in the integrity of the company and you'll be proud to work with the support materials. You'll feel good about working with a company that has been in business over 30 years and never had a single piece of bad publicity. But you'll be especially proud to work with a product line that is superior to anything else now available.

4 You will LOVE the products! Not because you buy them to get a check, but because you won't think of spending a day without them. And because they are organic and environmentally sensitive, you'll feel good about what you're doing for the planet.

6 You'll be able to build your group (and thus, your checks) bigger – sooner. Because you are working with a professional sponsor and company, you get the benefit of having a complete duplicatable system to follow. Step-by-step – the entire program has been laid out for you. You and your entire organization have the same track to run on. You will get personal coaching for someone who has done it successfully.

8 You'll get the training and assistance you need to win. Because you'll be joining the organization of one of the best network marketers on the planet. You'll get help with presentations, 3 way calls, camera ready ads, demand conferencing and the chance to participate in ad co-ops like this.

9 You'll make what you're really worth! With the fairest compensation plan in the industry. There are no $100,000 poster boys (or girls) in this company. We have a balanced breakaway plan that allows the average distributor to make better than average incomes. And trips, contests, profit sharing, bonuses and other incentives that allow top producers to live a lifestyle that most can only dream about. We have more people driving new cars and earning over 5 grand a month than any company in the industry. Period.

10 Because you're tired of getting in on the ground floor – only to find out there's a basement. You've learned that the "hot" new deals of today aren't around tomorrow. You've been through that phase and now you're ready to build a business that will last your lifetime.

11 Because the suspense is killing you!

A FEW WORDS OF CAUTION:

It is only fair to warn you, this ad is not for everyone. In fact, its not for most people.

25,000 people will read this magazine. About 400 of them are the people we are looking for. How do you know if this program is right for you? Well, we can begin by finding out if it's not right for you.

If you are working a program now, have a sponsor who works with you, a good product at a fair price, the company is honest, but you've never made big dollars – our program is not for you. You have the elements necessary for success, just give it time. Calling us just to "check it out" will only distract you from what you should be doing – focusing on your business and forgetting everything else.

If you are working one or more programs, but are looking for a "complimentary" program or an "insurance" program, please keep looking. Our program only works for those who are loyal, focused and committed to working it exclusively. We don't need your money, and you wouldn't fit in.

If you would like a program that your sponsor will "build your downline for you," you're on the wrong page. Likewise, if you are seeking a program that will make you rich simply by mailing postcards.

Finally, please don't insult our intelligence (or yours) by calling to reverse us into looking at your program. We acutely scrutinized 83 programs before selecting this one. We wish you peace and good luck in your endeavors, and hope you will extend us the same courtesy.

However, if you fit none of the above descriptions, please continue.

We are not particularly concerned with your experience. We are more interested in your desire to succeed. If you are coachable, persistent, willing to learn a simple, proven system, and you are prepared to earn your success – then by all means, call the number below.

1-800-▪▪▪▪▪▪▪

NOTES

NOTES

NOTES

NOTES

NOTES

The Mechanics Of Marketing

"Better to send a poor package to a good list - than send an excellent package to a poor list."

"Your letter must be believable.   If it's not believable, your mailing will fail, even if it's true."

Getting the Envelope Open

- Use no return address.

- Hand-address the envelope.

- Use a commemorative stamp.

- Use a window envelope.

- Use a double-window envelope.

- Use different colored paper.

- Offer something FREE inside.

- Use an odd-sized envelope.

- Use two colors.

- Use teaser copy.

Questions to ask when Buying a Mailing List

1. What is the source of the list?

2. Is it a compiled or response list?

3. Are the responses by mail, phone, TV, radio or other?

4. How old is the list?

5. What kind of selection criteria is available?

6. What are the addressing alternatives?

7. Is a sample piece required?

8. Can the average size of the transaction made by individuals on the list be determined?

9. What is the policy on "nixies?"

10. When was the list cleaned last?

Which List to Mail?

You can mail 10,000 pieces to either list:

List A	List B
Has tested at 1.0% return	Has tested at 0.8% return
Costs $99 per thousand	Costs $49 per thousand

Variables that affect your mail list response rate

1. Quality of the names

2. Promotional copy

3. Quality of the promotional literature

4. The offer

5. Price

6. Mailing lead time

7. Ease of buying / responding

8. Frequency of use of a given set of names

9. Home vs. office address

10. The economy

11. Time of year

12. Unknown factors

Maintaining List Accuracy

2% a month move, retire or die.

Usually:

1-year old list = 75% accurate

2-year old list = 60% accurate

3-year old list = 50% accurate

Keeping an in-house list:

- Mail first-class occasionally.

- Build an "Audit Box" into the piece.

- Send out an audit flier.

- Include "Address Correction Requested" under your return address.

Case Study of a Mail Campaign

In gratitude for the tremendous value that John Fogg
and Upline have been to me, I offered to mail out an
endorsement letter to my database about the magazine.

I've enclosed the actual letter I sent him, including all
the enclosures, budgets, etc., for you to see.

There are a lot of lessons here for you:

>   Third-party endorsements

>   Up-selling

>   Back-end sales

>   Marginal net worth of a customer vs. cost of
>   getting one

>   Building value

>   Mailing profitably

>   Creating an irresistible offer

Randy Gage
Business Development Consultant

August 19, 1994

Upline
John Fogg
400 East Jefferson Street
Charlottesville, VA 22902

VIA FAX

My Dearest John Milton,

Enclosed you will find my endorsement letter and the budget for your mailing. I've given you costs for 5,000 pieces and 7,000. If money permits, I suggest you mail 2,000 with a different key code to another list such as Tom Schreiter's. This would give you an idea of what response my endorsement and offer might get from a list other than my own. I suspect it would still pull respectable. I recommend you ask Tom what he thinks.

Also, you've asked me to do the impossible: i.e. - to project what I think this mailing will do. Anyway, here's my guesstimate: 5,000 pieces at 1.25% = 62 subscriptions. Normally, I would project 2% for an offer this strong to my list, but keep in mind many of my better buyers are probably already subscribers. Anyone on my "hot list" (bought in the last 90 days) has already received an Upline offer from me - many of which have bought it as you know. In any event, that should bring you back $4,300. That should help to defray your out-of-pocket expenses.

However it's critical that the new subscribers immediately get a letter from you a) confirming they made a good investment, and b) offering them an incentive to share Upline with their group. One week later (right after they've received their first issue) they need to get your catalog in an envelope with a cover letter re-stating the value and perhaps a premium for ordering something within 7 days. I've enclosed the letters we use for my Voiceletter subscriptions, after seminars, and with our catalog. Hopefully they will be of help to you.

7501 East Treasure Drive, Lobby Floor, North Bay Village, FL 33141, (305) 864-6658

For the most part, my database is people with groups from 5 to 5,000. If you repeat the same process with the new subs you get from the bounce-back letter it's quite conceivable for you to generate 500 subscriptions over the next year from the initial 62.

Also, I would encourage you to punch up the "New Resources" section of your publication. This should be a considerable source of back-end income for you. I don't know the Marginal Net Worth of your readers to you, but I think this, combined with your Resource Catalog should bring you a very profitable mailing indeed. Please let me know what you think.

Warmly,

Randy

MAIL OUT BUDGET

	5,000 pcs.	7,000 pcs.
POSTAGE	$1,000	$1,400
PRINTING & TYPESETTING	$1,500	$1,850
MAIL HOUSE	$850	$1,150
MAIL LIST	_____	???
	$3,350	$4,400

With Catalog

Here's the Money Making Catalog You Requested!!!

Dear Colleague,

You asked for it and here it is: My latest SMALL & HOME BASED BUSINESS SUCCESS CATALOG. Use it to position yourself at the top levels of success. This catalog is the most comprehensive resource available for getting more sales and making more money in your business.

Would you like to appear on radio, television and receive scads of publicity - all for FREE? **Get the special Free publicity combination offer on page 8.**

Doctors, lawyers, accountants, brokers: Would you like to promote your business with talk programs and seminars? Then you need the COMMUNICATION CASH album featured on page 2.

Want to write ads, flyers, brochures and letters that sell **more products or services NOW? Then you need CASH COPY on page 11.** Get it.

Networkers: Are you tired of having so many drop-outs? Put the GET STARTED materials on page 15 to work for you. This system has taken 80% of what used to be drop-outs - and turned them into productive distributors.   Would you like to have a steady stream of new prospects for your business?   Check out SPECIAL REPORTS number 7, 10 and 15.

All told, there's over 75 success tools that will help you build your business faster and make deliciously outrageous incomes.

Stop wasting your time and money. **Start** making the money you're capable of. If you order by credit card, you can call now and have the materials you need in just a few days.   If you want more income now - give yourself the tools you need to get the job done.

Yours for success,

Randy Gage

P.S. Don't forget that if you need urgent, personalized attention, that I can consult for you on a hourly, monthly retainer or per project basis. Also, call now if you would like to bring me to your area. While the rest of the year is booked, we do have a limited number of dates left for the Spring.

August 19, 1994

Seminar Graduation

GOOD MORNING CHRIS!

    Congratulations on your graduation from "Record Setting Sales." I hope you were pleased with the seminar. Let me take this opportunity to offer my heartfelt gratitude for the wonderful response I received.

    As you know, Randy Gage and I are publishing a Sales and Marketing Successletter beginning next month. The regular price is $95 per year. If you would like a charter subscription, call 1-800-432-4243 and we will reserve you a copy. As a special promotion, you will only pay $39 if you call this week - a savings of $56.

    I'm looking forward to a long, successful sales relationship with you. I am committed to your success, and I can't wait to return to Houston!

Warmly,

Dale Ledbetter

DL/dp

August 19, 1994

GOOD MORNING JIM!

     I wanted to take a minute to drop you a personal note to wel-
come you to the Dynamic Action Voiceletter. I'm excited that you
have decided to become a part of this program. I grateful to have
the opportunity to spend 60 minutes a month in your life.

     I encourage you to put the Voiceletter to the most use pos-
sible. Have your network over and play the tapes as part of your
training program. And be sure to take them along as you drive -
turn your car into a "university on wheels."

     If you think of areas you would like to see discussed in the
months ahead, please be sure to let me know.

     You should be getting your first issue in a few days if you
haven't already. Thanks again for the opportunity to work with you
monthly. I will strive to provide you with bold, dynamic options,
and up to the minute information to help you on your way towards
networking Success. Have a better than Dynamic Day!

Your Networking Coach,

Randy Gage

RG/da

The Printer

14278·14286 BISCAYNE BLVD.
NORTH MIAMI BEACH, FLORIDA 33181
TEL. (305) 947-9700   FAX (305) 947-4060
DIVISION OF AMERICAN SPECIALTY SALES CORP

QUOTATION
VALID FOR 30 DAYS

CUSTOMER ___ G R & D I ___   DATE __ 8/17/94 __

ADDRESS _____   TEL. _____

                                 FAX _____

| CUST. P.O.# | | JOB NAME Letterhd + Env. | | TERMS: COD ☐ OPEN ☐ |
| PROOF DUE | FAX | JOB DUE: | NO PROOF REQUIRED ☐ | CAMERA READY ☐ |

If customer does not want a proof, *The Printer* is not responsible for printing errors.

SIGNATURE OF CLIENT _____   ORDERED BY _____

QUANT.	DESCRIPTION	UNIT PRICE	AMOUNT
5000	8½ x 11 Letter 2 Col-		1400 —
"	1 Col		
"	2 Col		
"	10/24 Env 1 Col.		
7000	8½ x 11 Letter 2 Col		1750 —
"	1 Col		
"	2 Col.		
"	10/24 Env 1 Col		
	(Green Linen Available)		

☐ TYPESET	☐ PASTEUP (layout)	☐ MECHANICAL		
☐ STAPLE	☐ ARTWORK	☐ STAT/HALFTONE ☐ CHANGES		
☐ FOLD	☐ CUTTING	☐ PADDING ☐		
☐ COLOR INK	☐ COLLATE	☐ NUMBER From ___ to ___	SUB TOTAL	
			TAX	
			TOTAL	
			DEPOSIT	
			SHIPPING	
			BALANCE	

RANDY GAGE
7501 East Treasure Drive
North Bay Village, FL 33141
G-13#

CRITICALLY IMPORTANT

RANDY GAGE
Business Development Consultant

**Ref: The one resource you'd never
forgive me for not telling you about . . .**

Dear Colleague,

I have never written a letter of this kind before. I doubt very seriously if I will ever write one again. But I value you so much as a client that I would feel remiss if I did not bring this to your attention.

When someone produces something that is <u>a quantum leap</u> above what everyone else in the industry is doing - it deserves to be supported. By me, by you, and by everyone who believes in and is working toward the long term advocacy of the network marketing profession.

There is just such a thing right now . . .

It's called **UpLine** and there's never been anything quite like it to build your business. It's the monthly journal for network marketing <u>professionals.</u> And it comes to you from John Fogg, author of *The Greatest Networker in the World.* Which as you know, is a book I've been championing since the day it came out. If you've read it then you know the quality of material John produces. If you don't know, ask someone.

Well John is the editor of UpLine. And each month he assembles some of the greatest talent in network marketing to help you grow your business.

You learn where to find leaders, how to turn prospects into distributors faster, how to make more money with retail sales and just all-around how to build your group (and thus your check) bigger - faster. It would be no hype and no exaggeration to say that the information in one issue can make you hundreds or even thousands of dollars extra. Back when I was still building organizations I credit UpLine with making me an extra $30,000. Jim Kossert, who's a Presidential Director with Enrich figures UpLine made him at least ten grand extra last year.

So you can see why I'm writing such an unprecedented letter. I'm not only endorsing UpLine, but I'm downright pleading with you to get yourself a subscription NOW!

1

G164

Why am I so insistent?

Especially when I don't make a dime off it? Two reasons. Number one - because you've attended one of my programs or used my materials, you're a valued client. I feel like I owe it to you to tell you about something that can make such a difference in your business. Secondly, when someone produces a resource to support the industry of the caliber of UpLine - I believe we all should all shout it to the rooftops.

What's it worth to you?

I don't know. If you're the type of person who does MLM as a hobby and you want to make an extra $30 a month - UpLine is probably over your head. However, if you're looking to networking for complete financial independence, or at least a significant second income - then UpLine is exactly what you need. The knowledge you get can make you thousands or even tens of thousands of dollars.

Every issue brings you training articles from some of the best in the business (you know who included), interviews with top industry earners, success profiles and much more. On top of that, you get money making insights from people outside the industry like financial wizard Charles Givens, noted economist Paul Zane Pilzer and sales gurus like Zig Ziglar and Dale Ledbetter.

Every serious networker I know in the industry not only subscribes to UpLine, but they make sure every one of their key people do as well. Randall Anderson, the Chairman of Oxyfresh requires it as part of their Leadership Development Program. This makes sure the valuable knowledge they get is carried down through their entire organization.

Three other things. They're important.

First, as a subscriber to UpLine you get exclusive copyright privileges. You may reproduce anything you read in UpLine for training, prospecting, articles in your own newsletter, etc. Just doing this with one article is worth the price of a year's subscription!

Second, you should know, there are no ads in UpLine. Period. No endorsement, on "company of the month," no "this is the program I work" nonsense. This is a totally generic, unbiased overview of the entire industry. The kind of tool you will wholeheartedly recommend to your entire organization.

And finally, you can save a lot of money on prospecting and training tools. Because UpLine publishes a Resource Catalog with subscriber discounts on materials by people like Tom Schreiter, John Kalench and myself. Because they are a dealer - they buy in massive quantities and pass the savings along to you, their subscriber. For example, my "How to Earn at Least $100,000 . . . " album (which you likely bought from me for $69) you can get from UpLine at $59!

2

G164

What all this cost?

Too cheap. Really. Personally, I'd charge a couple of hundred a year for this kind of newsletter/magazine/money-making-resource. But John insists on giving it away at the ridiculous low price of only $69 <u>for a one year subscription!</u> ($79 for foreign countries.) You may purchase a lifetime subscription for just $1,000. So I strongly recommend you order now before he follows my advice and raises the price.

But there's even more . . .

I already told you, I don't get anything for this. Instead, I've asked John to sweeten the deal for you. If you order within the next 7 days, you'll get a copy of **The Greatest Networker in the World** personally autographed by John and a copy of **MONEY, MONEY, MONEY, MONEY, MONEY**, the savvy new prospecting tool from UpLine.

What's next?

Call UpLine at **1-800-800-6349**. You can put your subscription on VISA, MC or AMEX, or you may send a check or money order to: **UpLine, 400 E. Jefferson Street, Charlottesville, VA 22902.** Please do it within 7 days so you receive the two free books.

Oh, and I almost forgot . . . John takes all the risk!

Here's John's guarantee: Use UpLine to build your business for one entire year, **If you don't feel it made you more successful - tell them - and they will return your entire $69, no hard feelings.** Really. And keep the two free books for your trouble.

I don't mind telling you - with a better-than-risk-free offer like that . . . . I think you'd have to be nuts not to subscribe if you're at all serious about your network marketing career.

Warmly,

Randy Gage

Randy Gage

P.S. I know many of you already get UpLine because I've been recommending it for a while. And if you've still read this far, either I write great love letters, or you need a life! Either way, you deserve a reward. So I asked John, and he's agreed, to give you the same deal for your next year's renewal as long as you call within the required 7 days. Reach them now at 1-800-800-6349.

G164

NOTES

NOTES

SECTION

11

Using Technology To Build Faster

VOICEMAIL SYSTEM

- Very good for duplication
- Saves tons of time
- Keeps communication flowing through proper sponsorship lines

CONFERENCE CALLS

- Once a month ideal if you use voicemail - weekly if you don't
- Design with the prospect in mind
- Reaffirm training - don't use to introduce new training usually

DEMAND CONFERENCES

- A permanent taped conference call
- Change frequently
- Keep fast-paced and upbeat

FAX-ON-DEMAND

- Better if run by the company

- Helps support long distance lines

SATELLITES

- Best if provided by the company

- Best used for training - not very duplicatable yet for prospecting

COMPUTERS / INTERNET

- Not very duplicatable yet

- Eventually will take over the communications role played by phones, FAX, and voicemail

NOTES

NOTES

SECTION

12

Designing Your Marketing Plan

I FOLLOW THE TREND

- Network marketing $70 - $100 billion a year in sales.
- Practiced in all 50 states and over 75 countries and territories around the world.
- Establish 500,000 jobs a year eliminated by technology.

II CHOOSE THE KIND OF BUSINESS YOU WANT

- Big cash quickly or long-term residual.
  - Cold Market = Fast, Larger Investment, Big $ Quicker
  - Warm Market = Steady, Duplicatable, Bigger $ Long Term
- Achieve the right balance for you and the group you want.

III SET YOUR GOALS

- Set your 2-4 year plan and regress backward.
- Determine how many people you need to sponsor.
- Determine how many presentations you need to make.

IV MAKE YOUR ACTION PLAN

- Build from hot to cold.
- Use *Mastering Marketing Fundamentals* as a checklist.

V GO OUT AND GET STARTED!!!

How to Earn at Least $100,000 a Year in Network Marketing audiotape album by Randy Gage

How to Earn at Least $100,000 a Year in Network Marketing Study Guide by Randy Gage

Powerline Systems Network Marketing Planner

Tom Schreiter's *Big Al* book series

Street Smart Networking, book by Robert Butwin

Big Al's MLM Sponsoring Secrets, by Tom Schreiter

Long Distance Builder's Kit, by Randy Gage

Being the Best You Can Be in MLM, book by John Kalench

17 Secrets of the Master Prospectors, book by John Kalench

Build Your Vision, by John Kalench

Dynamic Development Series, by Randy Gage

NOTES

NOTES